AF316927

CREATING VALUE

Winning Customer Loyalty and Trust

Nurudeen Adeola Akande

Table Of Contents

PREFACE

In a world where competition is fierce, customer expectations are constantly shifting, and technology is reshaping the way businesses interact with consumers, one fundamental truth remains unchanged: businesses that prioritize value creation, trust, and loyalty outperform those that don't.

Every day, businesses across different industries struggle to gain market share, attract new customers, and sustain profitability. Many rely on aggressive marketing campaigns, price wars, or short-term promotional tactics to stay ahead. While these strategies might yield temporary gains, they often fail to create the long-term success that every business owner aspires to achieve. The real secret to business longevity lies in creating meaningful value, building trust, and securing customer loyalty.

I have spent years observing how some businesses thrive while others fail. The most successful brands are not necessarily the ones with the biggest budgets or the flashiest advertisements. Instead, they are the ones that have mastered the art of consistently exceeding customer expectations, fostering emotional connections, and delivering exceptional experiences. These businesses understand that trust and loyalty are earned, not bought.

But what exactly does it mean to create value? And how does value translate into customer trust and loyalty? Many businesses make the mistake of assuming that value is purely about the quality of their product or service. While that is important, value is also about understanding customers deeply, knowing their needs, desires, and pain points and ensuring that every interaction adds to their satisfaction. It is about building authentic relationships, treating customers as people rather than transactions, and making them feel seen, heard, and valued. True value comes from delivering experiences that go beyond expectations, creating a lasting impression that extends beyond a single purchase. It is also about transparency being honest and open, even when things go wrong because nothing damages trust faster than deception or inconsistency.

At the heart of value creation is a culture of trust, not just between businesses and customers, but within organizations themselves. A company cannot deliver value externally if it does not first instill a sense of trust, integrity, and accountability among its employees. Leadership plays a crucial role in this, setting the tone for how customers are treated and ensuring that every member of the organization understands the importance of prioritizing the customer experience. When businesses foster an internal culture rooted in value creation, that mindset naturally extends to their external relationships, strengthening their credibility and long-term success.

This book, *Creating Value: Winning Customer Loyalty and Trust*, is structured to take you on a journey through the core principles of value creation. It is designed for entrepreneurs, business leaders, marketers, customer service professionals, and anyone who wants to build a brand that truly matters. Throughout these ten chapters, we will explore why trust and loyalty matter more than ever in today's business world, how to develop a deep understanding of your customers, and the power of transparency, communication, and emotional connection in business. We will also examine how to exceed customer expectations and create memorable experiences, the role of leadership in fostering a value-driven company culture, and the ways in which digital transformation is shaping customer trust and brand perception. More importantly, this book will provide practical, actionable steps to secure long-term customer loyalty, ensuring that businesses are not only attracting customers but also keeping them engaged and satisfied.

This is not just another business book filled with theories and abstract ideas. It is a practical guide backed by real-world examples, case studies, and strategies that can be applied immediately. My goal is to help you rethink how you approach business moving away from short-term transactions to long-term, trust-based relationships that create real impact.

No matter the size of your business or the industry you operate in, the ability to win customer trust and foster loyalty is your greatest asset. If you can master this, you will not only gain a competitive edge but also build a brand that people love, respect, and remain loyal to for years to come.

It is my hope that as you read this book, you will begin to see value creation as more than just a strategy. It is a philosophy, a mindset, and a commitment to putting customers at the heart of everything you do. Let's embark on this journey together and discover how creating value can transform your business, your brand, and your customer relationships.

FOREWORD

In an era where businesses rise and fall at an unprecedented pace, one thing remains constant: the companies that succeed are those that understand the profound impact of value creation. Customers today are more informed, more discerning, and less forgiving than ever before. They no longer remain loyal to businesses out of habit; they seek brands that genuinely serve their needs, respect their time, and align with their values. The challenge, then, is no longer just about attracting customers but about keeping them—building relationships founded on trust, credibility, and unwavering commitment to delivering value.

In *Creating Value: Winning Customer Loyalty and Trust*, Nurudeen Adeola Akande unpacks the timeless yet often overlooked principles of what it truly means to build a customer-first business. This book is not just about selling products or services, it is about creating meaningful experiences that leave a lasting impression. Through compelling insights, practical strategies, and real-world examples, the author takes readers on a transformative journey, offering a roadmap to business success that is built not on gimmicks or quick wins but on substance and sustainability.

Over the years, I have witnessed businesses pour millions into advertising campaigns, only to lose customers because they failed to deliver what truly mattered. The truth is, no amount of marketing can compensate for a lack of value. Customers are not deceived by catchy slogans or empty promises; they see through the noise and gravitate towards brands that make a real difference in their lives. That is precisely why this book is so timely and essential. It is a reminder that businesses do not thrive by chance; they thrive because they consistently provide solutions, inspire trust, and foster connections that go beyond transactions.

What sets this book apart is its practicality. Many business books focus on abstract theories or broad generalizations, but Nurudeen Adeola Akande understands that true value lies in action. The principles shared in these pages are not just concepts, they are strategies that can be implemented by anyone, from small business owners and startup founders to executives leading multinational corporations. Whether you are trying to build brand loyalty, establish credibility, or navigate the complexities of digital customer engagement, this book provides the tools and insights you need to succeed.

Another powerful aspect of this book is its emphasis on trust as a competitive advantage. In an age where consumer skepticism is at an all-time high, the ability to earn and maintain trust is what separates businesses that endure from those that fade into obscurity. Trust is not given; it is earned through consistency, integrity, and an unwavering commitment to excellence. Businesses that prioritize trust do not just retain customers; they create advocates, people who willingly spread the word, defend the brand in times of crisis, and become lifelong supporters.

As you turn the pages of this book, you will find more than just strategies; you will find a new way of thinking about business; one that challenges the status quo and redefines what it means to win in today's competitive landscape. If you are looking for a blueprint to not just attract customers but to keep them, to not just generate sales but to build relationships, then you are holding the right book in your hands.

It is with great excitement and confidence that I recommend *Creating Value: Winning Customer Loyalty and Trust* to anyone who wants to build a business that is not only profitable but also meaningful. This book is an essential read for those who believe that success is not measured by numbers alone but by the impact they create in the lives of their customers.

INTRODUCTION

In the ever-evolving world of business, one principle remains unchanged: customers are the lifeblood of every organization. No matter how innovative a product is, how compelling a marketing campaign appears, or how competitive a pricing model might be, a business cannot survive let alone thrive without customers who believe in its value and are willing to return. However, in an age where consumer loyalty is fleeting and trust is difficult to earn, the real challenge lies not just in attracting customers but in keeping them.

Many businesses today operate under the mistaken belief that value creation is limited to the products or services they offer. While delivering high-quality goods is important, true value extends far beyond the physical or functional aspects of a product. It is about the entire experience a customer has with a brand from the first interaction to the last. It is about solving problems, meeting expectations, and ultimately creating something that customers find indispensable.

This book, *Creating Value: Winning Customer Loyalty and Trust*, is built on the fundamental idea that businesses do not win by being the loudest or the cheapest; they win by being the most valuable. The companies that stand the test of time are those that focus on consistent excellence, meaningful engagement, and a deep understanding of their customers' evolving needs. Businesses that prioritize short-term profits at the expense of trust may see temporary success, but they rarely achieve long-term sustainability.

The concept of value creation is not new, but it is often misunderstood. Many businesses think value is about adding more features to a product, offering discounts, or investing in expensive advertising campaigns. While these strategies can attract attention, they do not necessarily build loyalty. Value is about understanding what matters most to customers and consistently delivering on those expectations. It is about making every customer interaction count, creating memorable experiences, and standing for something beyond mere profit.

One of the biggest mistakes businesses make is assuming that customer loyalty is automatic. The reality is that customers today have endless choices and little patience for mediocrity. The moment they feel unappreciated or disappointed, they will move on to a competitor. Trust, once broken, is incredibly difficult to regain. This is why value creation must be intentional—it requires a proactive approach to customer engagement, a commitment to excellence, and a willingness to adapt.

This book is structured into ten chapters, each addressing a critical aspect of value creation. It begins by exploring the foundations of customer trust and loyalty, then delves into understanding customer behavior, exceeding expectations, and leveraging authenticity as a competitive advantage. We will examine how businesses can build lasting relationships with customers, how leadership and company culture influence customer perceptions, and why digital transformation has reshaped how brands establish trust in today's hyperconnected world. Each chapter provides real-world case studies, practical insights, and actionable strategies designed to help businesses implement the principles of value creation effectively.

Whether you are an entrepreneur, a business executive, a startup founder, or a customer service professional, the lessons in this book will equip you with the knowledge to not just attract customers, but to build lasting relationships that translate into business growth and stability. The insights shared are drawn from extensive research, industry case studies, and personal observations of what works and what doesn't when it comes to customer trust and loyalty.

As you read through these chapters, I encourage you to think about your own business or brand. How are you creating value today? How do your customers perceive your brand? Are you prioritizing long-term trust over short-term gains? These are the questions that separate businesses that merely exist from those that truly thrive and make an impact.

The key takeaway from this book is simple: businesses that focus on delivering genuine value, building trust, and fostering customer loyalty will always have a competitive edge. In a market flooded with choices, the brands that succeed are the ones that customers trust, respect, and feel a connection with.

CHAPTER ONE

THE FOUNDATION OF VALUE CREATION

In the world of business, value is often misunderstood. Many companies assume that value is simply the quality of their product or service, but value goes far beyond that. It is the sum total of how a business makes its customers feel, the problems it solves, and the lasting impact it creates in their lives. Businesses that truly understand value creation recognize that it is not just about what they offer but about how their customers perceive what they offer.

Value is subjective. What one customer sees as valuable might be different from another. A luxury car brand may see value in high-end craftsmanship and exclusivity, while a budget airline may define value as affordability and convenience. In both cases, the businesses succeed because they deeply understand what their customers want, and they deliver it consistently. At its core, value creation is about meeting and exceeding customer expectations. It is about giving people a reason to choose your business over competitors—not just once, but again and again. When businesses fail to create value, they become irrelevant. Customers today have endless choices, and if a business does not provide meaningful value, customers will have no hesitation in walking away.

Customers do not engage with businesses blindly. Every interaction they have with a brand is influenced by expectations—whether they are conscious of them or not. Expectations are shaped by many factors, including past experiences, word-of-mouth recommendations, advertising, industry standards, and personal preferences. When a customer walks into a restaurant, they expect good food, reasonable service, and a pleasant atmosphere. When they buy a smartphone, they expect reliability, ease of use, and value for their money. If a business meets these expectations, the customer is satisfied. If it exceeds expectations, the customer becomes loyal. But if a business falls short, it creates disappointment, and in today's digital age, disappointed customers do not remain silent. They share their experiences through online reviews, social media, and word of mouth, which can significantly damage a brand's reputation.

Businesses that succeed in value creation do not just react to customer expectations—they anticipate and shape them. They know that trust is built when expectations are consistently met or exceeded. Trust, in turn, is the foundation of customer loyalty. To create value effectively, businesses must focus on three fundamental pillars: relevance, differentiation, and consistency. A business that lacks relevance will struggle to attract customers in the first place. A business that lacks differentiation will find itself in a race to the bottom, constantly competing on price. And a business that lacks consistency will never build the trust needed for long-term loyalty.

Apple is one of the most valuable companies in the world, not just because it sells high-quality products but because it has mastered the art of value creation. Apple understands that value is not just about technology, it is about the experience, the ecosystem, and the brand perception it has cultivated over decades. Apple customers do not just buy iPhones because of their technical specifications. They buy iPhones because they trust Apple to deliver a seamless, intuitive experience that integrates perfectly with their other devices. They buy into the brand promise of innovation, simplicity, and exclusivity. Apple creates value by making its customers feel like they are part of something special. Every Apple product launch is an event. Every Apple store is designed to offer a unique retail experience. The company invests heavily in customer service and after-sales support, ensuring that customers always feel valued. Apple does not just sell phones or laptops, it sells an identity, a lifestyle, and a sense of belonging. That is what real value creation looks like.

Despite the importance of value creation, many businesses fail to get it right. Some focus too much on features instead of benefits, forgetting that customers do not just buy products for their specifications; they buy them for the problems they solve and the emotions they evoke. Others fail to understand customer needs, ignoring feedback or resisting change, which ultimately makes them irrelevant in the market. Many businesses struggle with consistency, delivering great experiences one day and terrible ones the next, leaving customers frustrated and skeptical. Some companies compete solely with price, assuming that being the cheapest is the only way to attract customers, but in reality, customers are often willing to pay more for brands they trust and respect. One of the most overlooked aspects of value creation is emotional connection. Customers are more likely to remain loyal to brands they feel connected to. Businesses that ignore this emotional component risk losing out to competitors who do it better.

The foundation of value creation begins with a customer-first mindset. Businesses must shift their perspective from "What do we want to sell?" to "What do our customers truly need?" This requires deep customer research, listening to feedback, and continuously improving based on insights. One of the simplest yet most powerful questions any business could ask itself is: "If we disappeared tomorrow, would our customers miss us?" If the answer is no, then the business has not created enough value. The brands that thrive are those that embed themselves so deeply in their customers' lives that they become irreplaceable.

The ability to create value is not just a strategy; it is a discipline. It requires an ongoing commitment to excellence, a deep understanding of customers, and a willingness to innovate continuously. Businesses that create real value are not only solving problems but are also shaping the way customers think, behave, and make decisions. Value creation is not static, it evolves as customer needs change, as technology advances, and as industries shift. This means that businesses cannot afford to be complacent. What was considered valuable yesterday may not hold the same relevance today, and what customers appreciate today may be insufficient tomorrow.

The evolution of value in business is evident in how industries have changed over time. Decades ago, simply having a quality product was enough to attract customers. But today, the landscape has shifted dramatically. Consumers are no longer just looking for quality; they want efficiency, convenience, personalization, and emotional connection. A brand that fails to adapt to these evolving expectations will inevitably lose its competitive edge. Consider the transformation of the retail industry. Brick-and-mortar stores were once the dominant force in commerce, but with the rise in e-commerce, convenience has become a driving factor in purchasing decisions. Companies like Amazon have revolutionized value creation by focusing on speed, efficiency, and ease of access. Customers are no longer willing to wait in long lines or travel to physical stores when they can have the same products delivered to their doorsteps in record time.

The same principle applies across different industries. In the financial sector, traditional banks once held a monopoly on financial services, but with the emergence of fintech companies, the definition of value has changed. Consumers now expect instant transactions, digital accessibility, and seamless user experiences. Banks that fail to offer mobile banking solutions or personalized financial products risk losing customers to more agile competitors. The ability to recognize these shifts and pivot accordingly is what separates businesses that remain relevant from those that fade into obscurity.

Creating value is also about removing friction. Customers naturally gravitate toward businesses that make their lives easier, solve their problems faster, and provide seamless experiences. This is why companies that eliminate unnecessary steps in their processes or streamline interactions often build the strongest customer relationships. A great example is how ride-hailing services like Uber and Bolt transformed the transportation industry. Before these platforms existed, getting a taxi was often a frustrating experience, customers had to find a taxi stand, negotiate fares, and deal with inconsistent service. Uber eliminated these pain points by introducing a digital solution that allowed users to book a ride within seconds, track their driver, and pay effortlessly through an app. The core service and transportation remained the same, but the way value was delivered changed entirely.

Consistency is another critical component of value creation. Customers do not just judge businesses based on a single interaction; they evaluate them based on how consistently they deliver on their promises. A restaurant that serves excellent food one day but delivers a poor experience the next will struggle to retain loyal customers. A fashion brand that releases high-quality products initially but later compromises on material quality will find its customer base shrinking over time. This is why some of the most successful brands in the world have rigorous standards in place to ensure uniformity in customer experience. Whether a customer shops at an Apple store in New York or Tokyo, the experience is designed to be seamless and familiar. Whether someone orders a Big Mac in Lagos or London, McDonald's ensures that the product meets the same taste and quality expectations. Customers appreciate businesses they can rely on, and consistency breed trust.

Beyond consistency, another factor that influences value creation is perceived value versus actual value. Businesses sometimes fall into the trap of assuming that the features they prioritize are what customers value the most, only to realize that customers perceive value differently. A hotel, for example, may invest heavily in luxury room designs, but if its check-in process is slow and its customer service is poor, guests will not perceive the hotel as valuable. On the other hand, a mid-range hotel that prioritizes fast service, cleanliness, and friendly staff may be perceived as offering more value even if its rooms are not as luxurious. The key takeaway here is that businesses must align what they think is valuable with what customers actually find valuable. The gap between actual value and perceived value is often what makes the difference between a thriving business and a struggling one.

Businesses that focus on long-term value creation also understand the importance of emotional engagement. Customers do not just buy products; they buy into stories, experiences, and a sense of belonging. This is why storytelling has become such a powerful tool in modern marketing. Brands that successfully weave narratives into their messaging often create deeper emotional connections with their audience. A brand like Nike, for instance, does not just sell athletic shoes, it sells motivation, determination, and the spirit of achievement. Its marketing campaigns rarely focus solely on product specifications; instead, they highlight stories of athletes overcoming obstacles, pushing their limits, and breaking barriers. This emotional connection makes customers feel aligned with the brand's values, which in turn fosters long-term loyalty.

Customer advocacy is the natural result of businesses that create value consistently. When customers experience genuine value, they do not just remain loyal, they become brand ambassadors. They share their experiences with friends, leave positive reviews, and defend the brand when it faces criticism. This kind of organic marketing is far more powerful than any paid advertising campaign. Word-of-mouth recommendations remain one of the strongest drivers of business growth because people trust real experiences more than corporate messaging. A business that focuses on value creation does not need to beg for testimonials or force engagement; satisfied customers willingly promote the brand because they believe in it.

As businesses grow, the challenge of maintaining value creation at scale becomes more complex. A startup that delivers outstanding customer service when it has 100 customers may struggle to maintain the same level of service when it expands to 10,000 customers. This is why businesses must continuously refine their processes, invest in customer relationship management, and develop systems that allow them to scale without compromising the quality of experience. Scaling value creation is not just about growing revenue; it is about ensuring that as a business expands, it continues to meet the expectations of its growing customer base.

Ultimately, the brands that succeed in value creation do not see it as an add-on to their business strategy; they see it as the foundation of everything they do. Value is not just created at the point of sale, it is embedded in customer service, branding, product development, leadership, company culture, and even in the way employees are treated. A company that values its employees is more likely to have employees who, in turn, value its customers. The philosophy of value creation is holistic, it extends beyond just products and services to encompass the entire ecosystem of a business.

1.1 The Role of Leadership in Value Creation

The foundation of value creation is not just built at the customer level, it begins at the very top, with leadership. A business's ability to create value is deeply rooted in its leadership philosophy and the decisions made at the highest levels. Leaders who prioritize long-term value over short-term profits set the tone for the entire organization. They create a culture where employees understand that their primary role is not just to sell products or services but to serve customers in a way that fosters loyalty and trust.

Great leaders recognize that value is not only delivered through the product or service itself but also through the internal workings of the company. They understand that value creation starts with how employees are treated, how internal systems operate, and how well the company's mission aligns with customer expectations. Companies with strong leadership in value creation ensure that every department, whether it is sales, customer service, product development, or even finance—functions with a customer-centric approach.

A compelling example of leadership-driven value creation is Amazon. Jeff Bezos built Amazon on the principle of customer obsession, ensuring that every major decision considered the customer's perspective first. Amazon's leadership instilled a mindset that prioritizes speed, convenience, and reliability in every business function. From developing one-click purchasing to investing in warehouse automation for faster deliveries, every innovation was driven by the goal of making life easier for customers. Amazon's leadership did not just focus on making profits, they focused on making Amazon indispensable to its customers.

On the other hand, companies with weak leadership often struggle to create value consistently. When leadership is focused purely on short-term financial performance, customer satisfaction tends to take a back seat. Cost-cutting measures may lead to reduced service quality, untrained staff, and a lack of investment in innovation. Over time, such businesses lose their competitive advantage because they fail to build long-term customer trust. This is why companies that experience frequent leadership changes, unclear business vision, or a toxic work culture often struggle with inconsistent value delivery.

Strong leaders not only drive value creation through innovation and customer experience but also through employee engagement. Employees who feel valued, empowered, and aligned with a company's mission are more likely to contribute positively to the customer experience. When employees are disengaged or feel undervalued, it directly affects their interactions with customers. A disengaged employee at a customer service desk, for example, will not go the extra mile to resolve an issue, which in turn affects customer perception of the brand.

The key takeaway is that businesses that create real, lasting value are led by visionaries who understand that value creation starts internally before it manifests externally. Companies that invest in leadership development, clear company vision, and a strong organizational culture find it easier to embed value into every aspect of their operations.

1.2 The Connection Between Brand Trust and Value Creation

Trust is one of the most powerful currencies in business today. Customers do not just buy from brands they recognize; they buy from brands they trust. Value creation and trust go hand in hand one cannot exist without the other. A business may have the best product on the market, but if customers do not trust the brand behind it, they will hesitate to engage.

Trust is built over time through consistency, transparency, and authenticity. Customers trust businesses that keep their promises, respond to concerns promptly, and maintain high ethical standards. Businesses that overpromise and underdeliver often struggle to retain trust, and once trust is lost, rebuilding it is incredibly difficult. This is why businesses that are reactive, only addressing customer issues when they arise, fail to establish deep trust with their audience.

Proactive businesses, on the other hand, build trust before customers even need reassurance.

Transparency is one of the fastest ways to earn trust. Customers appreciate brands that are open about their processes, pricing, and even mistakes. Businesses that try to hide flaws or manipulate customer perceptions often suffer serious backlash when the truth eventually surfaces. In contrast, companies that take responsibility for their errors, communicate openly, and work to rectify mistakes often earn even more trust than before. A great example is how some airlines handle flight delays. An airline that keeps passengers informed, provides compensation when necessary, and shows empathy for the inconvenience earns more customer loyalty than one that simply ignores complaints and makes no effort to acknowledge its shortcomings.

Another crucial element of trust-building is customer empowerment. Businesses that empower their customers, whether through clear return policies, strong customer support, or educational resources, strengthen their relationships with them. Take the example of fintech companies that provide financial literacy resources to their users. These companies do not just offer banking or investment services; they educate customers on how to make better financial decisions. This not only creates value but also establishes the company as a trusted authority in its space.

Brand trust is also closely tied to ethical business practices. Companies that engage in deceptive advertising, exploitative pricing, or unethical labor practices often find themselves losing customer trust rapidly. In today's world of social media activism and conscious consumerism, customers are more likely to call out businesses that engage in unethical behavior. Trustworthy brands, on the other hand, actively demonstrate corporate social responsibility, fair pricing, and a commitment to ethical practices.

One of the most telling signs of strong brand trust is when customers continue to support a business even in times of crisis. A company that has built a solid trust foundation can weather negative press, financial setbacks, and even product failures more effectively than one that has a weak trust relationship with its customers. For example, when Toyota faced recalls due to faulty accelerators, the company's long-standing commitment to safety and transparency helped it recover, as customers still believed in its overall brand integrity.

Value creation and trust are not separate concepts, they fuel each other. Businesses that create genuine value are rewarded with trust, and businesses that maintain trust are able to sustain long-term value creation. Trust is the glue that keeps customers loyal, ensuring that they choose a brand not just for a single purchase but for a lifetime.

As businesses navigate the complexities of today's competitive landscape, the importance of value-driven leadership, trust-building, and customer-centric innovation cannot be overstated. The most successful brands are those that recognize that value creation is not a destination but an ongoing process. It is a commitment to continuous improvement, a dedication to customer relationships, and an understanding that every touchpoint matters.

As industries continue to evolve, businesses must remain agile and proactive in reassessing their value propositions. The companies that thrive are those that do not just react to market changes but anticipate them, constantly aligning their strategies with shifting customer needs. Whether through strong leadership, a culture of consistency, transparency in operations, or the ability to build long-term trust, the brands that invest in value creation today will be the ones that stand strong in the future.

CHAPTER TWO

UNDERSTANDING YOUR CUSTOMERS

A Business cannot create meaningful value if it does not fully understand its customers. Customers are the foundation of every business, and their needs, desires, and expectations shape the way products and services should be designed, marketed, and delivered. Yet, many businesses operate under assumptions rather than insights, believing they know what customers want without actively listening or analyzing behavioral patterns. This is one of the biggest mistakes a business can make. True value creation begins with a deep and evolving understanding of customers, not just at the surface level but in ways that anticipate their evolving needs and expectations.

Understanding customers is more than just collecting demographic data such as age, income, and location. While these details are useful, they only scratch the surface. What truly drives purchasing decisions goes deeper customers make choices based on psychological, emotional, and practical factors. Two people with the same income level and age might have completely different motivations for choosing a product, making it crucial for businesses to dig deeper into customer psychology.

One of the key elements of understanding customers is recognizing that decision-making is not always rational. Many people assume that buyers logically weigh the pros and cons of a product before making a decision, but in reality, most decisions are driven by emotion, subconscious biases, and personal experiences. A luxury watch, for example, is not purchased simply because it tells time—customers buy it for status, craftsmanship, or even sentimental reasons. A fitness membership is not just about access to a gym, it is about motivation, self-discipline, and a sense of belonging. Companies that fail to recognize these deeper motivations often struggle to position their products in a way that resonates with their audience.

In today's fast-paced world, customers expect more than just products or services, they expect experiences. The way a brand interacts with them, the emotions it evokes, and the values it represents all influence their level of trust and engagement. Customers want to feel heard, valued, and understood. A company that listens to its customers, personalizes its approach, and continuously refines its offerings based on customer feedback will always be ahead of competitors who take a one-size-fits-all approach.

Many businesses fall into the trap of assuming that all customers are the same. They create generic marketing messages and uniform product offerings without considering that different customer segments have unique needs. The best companies recognize that their audience is made up of different buyer personas, each with specific pain points, desires, and expectations. For instance, a fashion brand that caters to working professionals, college students, and retirees cannot use the same messaging for all three groups. Each segment has different priorities, professionals might value sophistication and durability, students might seek affordability and trendiness, while retirees may prioritize comfort and quality. Businesses that understand these differences and tailor their offerings accordingly stand a better chance of building deeper relationships with their customers.

Another critical aspect of understanding customers is recognizing that customer behavior is constantly changing. What worked five years ago may not work today. Consumer habits evolve based on cultural shifts, technological advancements, and economic conditions. A clear example of this is how digital technology has transformed customer expectations. In the past, customers were willing to wait days for a response to their inquiries. Today, they expect instant communication through live chat, social media, and AI-powered customer support. Businesses that fail to adapt to these changing behaviors risk losing relevance.

Data analytics has become an indispensable tool for businesses looking to gain deeper insights into their customers. Companies no longer have to rely on guesswork; they can now track customer interactions, purchasing patterns, and engagement levels in real time. By analyzing this data, businesses can predict what customers might need before they even express it. For example, streaming platforms like Netflix and Spotify use algorithms to suggest content based on user preferences. These personalized recommendations create value by making the customer experience more relevant and convenient.

However, understanding customers goes beyond just analyzing data—it also requires active engagement and direct interaction. Businesses that truly listen to their customers by engaging in meaningful conversations, conducting surveys, and analyzing feedback gain a competitive advantage. Customer complaints, for instance, should not be seen as a nuisance but as valuable insights into areas that need improvement. Some of the best product innovations come from listening to what frustrates customers and addressing those pain points effectively.

One of the most powerful ways businesses can understand customers better is by putting themselves in the customer's shoes. This means experiencing their own products and services from the perspective of a customer. Many businesses make the mistake of designing systems, websites, or service processes based on internal convenience rather than customer ease. For example, a complicated checkout process on an e-commerce site may seem functional to developers but might be frustrating for customers who want a seamless, quick experience. Walking through the customer journey step by step allows businesses to identify pain points and areas that need improvement.

Trust plays a significant role in customer relationships, and trust is built on consistency. Customers want to know that they can rely on a brand to deliver a consistent experience every time they engage with it. This is why some of the most successful brands maintain uniform quality, service, and messaging across all touchpoints. Whether a customer visits a physical store, browses an online shop, or interacts with customer support, the experience should feel seamless and familiar. When customers see that a brand is dependable, their trust in it grows, leading to long-term loyalty.

Beyond transactions, businesses must recognize the importance of customer emotions in value creation. A customer who feels emotionally connected to a brand is far more likely to remain loyal than one who simply finds the product useful. Emotional connections are built through storytelling, brand authenticity, and shared values. A company that stands for something greater than just profits whether it is sustainability, social impact, or empowerment often resonates with customers. People want to support brands that align with their beliefs and values. This is why brands that authentically champion causes or engage in corporate social responsibility initiatives tend to have stronger customer loyalty.

In the modern marketplace, customers hold more power than ever before. They can shape brand reputations with a single review, influence purchasing decisions through social media, and demand higher standards of service. Businesses that fail to recognize this shift in power will struggle to maintain customer loyalty. Those that embrace it, however, will find that customers are not just buyers but partners in their brand's success. When customers feel valued, heard, and understood, they become more than just consumers, they become brand advocates who willingly promote the business through word-of-mouth and personal recommendations.

As businesses work to create value, they must remember that understanding the customer is an ongoing process, not a one-time effort. What customers expect today may not be what they expect in five years. Successful businesses are those that remain agile, continuously engage with their audience, and adjust their strategies to meet changing needs.

Customers are not just numbers on a sales report; they are individuals with unique needs, preferences, and expectations. The deeper a business understands its customers, the better it can tailor its offerings, communication, and overall experience. However, customer behavior is influenced by more than just logic, it is driven by psychology, emotions, and subconscious motivations. To truly understand customers, businesses must go beyond surface-level demographics and tap into the deeper psychological and behavioral patterns that shape purchasing decisions.

Customers do not always make purchasing decisions rationally. While traditional business models assume that buyers carefully evaluate their options before making a decision, the reality is that emotions, biases, and mental shortcuts often play a significant role. This is why two customers with similar financial means might make completely different choices when faced with the same product. One may be drawn to a brand because of nostalgia, while another may be influenced by peer recommendations or social status.

One of the key psychological principles that influence customer behavior is the concept of loss aversion. Studies show that people feel the pain of losing something more intensely than they feel the pleasure of gaining something. Businesses that understand this can frame their messaging in ways that highlight what customers stand to lose if they do not take action. For example, instead of saying, "Subscribe to our service for exclusive benefits," a company might say, "Don't miss out on exclusive benefits, subscribe today." The fear of missing out (FOMO) is a powerful motivator, and brands that understand this psychological trigger can craft messages that resonate more deeply.

Another powerful psychological factor is social proof. Customers tend to trust businesses that others have already validated. This is why testimonials, user reviews, and influencer endorsements are so effective. When people see that a product or service is being used and praised by others, they feel reassured that they are making a good decision. Businesses that leverage social proof effectively not only attract new customers but also reinforce the trust of existing ones.

Customers also respond to perceived effort and exclusivity. When something appears difficult to obtain, it is often seen as more valuable. This is why luxury brands limit product availability, and why invitation-only memberships create a sense of exclusivity. People value what they perceive as scarce or premium. Businesses that understand this can create demand not just through superior products but also by controlling the perception of accessibility.

Understanding customers also means recognizing that not all customers think alike. Different cultural backgrounds and generational influences shape how people perceive value, interact with brands, and make purchasing decisions. A strategy that works for one demographic might completely fail with another, which is why businesses must be mindful of how culture and generational differences shape customer behavior.

Cultural factors influence everything from communication styles to purchasing habits. In some cultures, customers expect a high level of personal interaction before making a purchase, while in others, self-service and automation are preferred. A business expanding into a new market must consider these differences carefully. A Western-style customer support model that relies on chatbots and self-service options may not work as well in regions where people expect personalized, human interaction. Businesses that fail to localize their approach risk alienating potential customers.

Generational differences also play a huge role in shaping expectations. Millennials and Gen Z customers, for example, place a high value on authenticity, social responsibility, and digital convenience. They are more likely to support brands that align with their values and are highly influenced by online content, peer recommendations, and digital experiences. They also expect businesses to be accessible across multiple channels, from social media to mobile apps.

In contrast, older generations may prioritize reliability, tradition, and personal service. They may be less likely to engage with a brand through digital platforms but more responsive to direct communication, loyalty programs, and in-person interactions. Businesses that cater to multiple generations must balance these varying expectations, ensuring that they provide both modern convenience and traditional customer service principles.

Understanding customers is not just about knowing why they buy, it is also about recognizing why they leave. Customer churn is one of the biggest challenges businesses faces, yet many companies fail to address it until it is too late. Most businesses assume that customers leave because of pricing issues or better offers from competitors, but studies show that the majority of customers leave because they feel unappreciated, unheard, or neglected.

One of the biggest mistakes businesses make is assuming that a lack of complaints means customer satisfaction. Many customers who are unhappy with a brand do not take the time to complain; they simply leave and never return. Worse still, they may share their negative experiences with others, damaging the brand's reputation. Businesses that wait until complaints arise before addressing customer dissatisfaction often lose valuable opportunities to retain customers.

To prevent silent churn, businesses must be proactive in gathering feedback. Regular customer check-ins, surveys, and engagement initiatives can help identify early warning signs before they escalate into full disengagement. Something as simple as a follow-up email after a purchase or a personalized thank-you message can make a customer feel valued and strengthen their connection to the brand.

Another reason customers leave is inconsistent experiences. A business that delivers excellent service once but fails to meet expectations the next creates uncertainty and frustration. Customers want to know that they can rely on a brand to deliver the same level of quality any time. When businesses focus too much on acquiring new customers but fail to maintain high standards for existing ones, the churn becomes inevitable.

Understanding customers is not just about analyzing their behaviors—it is about building meaningful connections. Customers today do not want to feel like just another transaction; they want to feel valued and understood. Businesses that take the time to build emotional connections with their audience create long-lasting relationships that extend beyond just the products or services they offer.

One way to build this connection is through storytelling. Brands that share authentic stories, whether about their origins, values, or customer success stories—create a sense of community and shared experience. Customers relate to brands that feel human, and businesses that use storytelling effectively can transform their messaging from a sales pitch into a conversation.

Another way to foster a deep connection is by making customers feel like partners in the brand's journey. This can be achieved through community engagement, loyalty programs, or user-generated content. Companies that involve customers in product development—by asking for feedback, co-creating designs, or beta testing new offerings, make them feel like stakeholders rather than passive buyers. When customers feel invested in a brand, their loyalty increases, and they become more likely to advocate for it.

A great example of customer co-creation is Lego Ideas, a platform where customers can submit their own Lego set designs. The best designs are turned into real products, and the creators receive a percentage of sales. This initiative not only fosters engagement but also strengthens customer loyalty by making them feel like part of the brand's creative process.

2.1 The Role of Trust in Customer Decision-Making

Trust is the invisible force that shapes customer relationships. It is not always explicitly acknowledged, but it is one of the most crucial factors in determining whether a customer chooses to engage with a brand or walks away. Trust is built through consistent and positive experiences, and once broken, it is incredibly difficult to rebuild. Businesses that fail to establish trust often find themselves struggling with customer retention, no matter how competitive their pricing or how impressive their product offerings may be.

Customers trust businesses that demonstrate competence, reliability, and honesty. Competence means that the product or service delivers exactly what it promises. A mobile phone brand, for instance, builds trust by ensuring its devices function smoothly, with good battery life and durability as advertised. Reliability means that the business consistently meets customer expectations over time. Customers need to feel confident that they will receive the same level of quality and service each time they engage with the brand. Honesty is about transparency—customers appreciate brands that communicate openly, admit mistakes when they happen, and take responsibility for rectifying them.

One of the key mistakes businesses make is assuming that trust is automatically granted. Trust is earned, and in today's marketplace, where customers are more skeptical than ever, businesses must actively work to gain and maintain it. This is particularly true in industries where customers have been repeatedly disappointed, such as the financial sector, where hidden fees and misleading contracts have caused widespread distrust. Companies in such industries must go the extra mile to prove their integrity through clear policies, fair pricing, and genuine customer care.

Social proof also plays a massive role in building trust. When potential customers see that others have had positive experiences with a business, they feel more confident in making a purchase. This is why reviews, testimonials, and word-of-mouth recommendations are so powerful. Many customers will not even consider engaging in a business if they do not see validation from other customers. Brands that highlight customer success stories, showcase authentic reviews, and encourage referrals create a trust ecosystem where customers feel secure in their purchasing decisions.

Another overlooked aspect of trust-building is predictability. Customers appreciate knowing what to expect. They value businesses that deliver on their promises, maintain a consistent level of service, and communicate clearly about policies, prices, and potential delays. When businesses constantly change their approach, shift pricing structures without explanation, or offer inconsistent service, trust erodes. A classic example of predictability in action is fast-food chains like McDonald's, where customers know exactly what they will get, no matter where they go. The brand may not offer the most gourmet dining experience, but its reliability creates a sense of trust that keeps customers returning.

Ultimately, trust is not built in a single interaction, it is cultivated over time. Every touchpoint a customer has with a brand, from the first website visit to after-sales support, contributes to their perception of trustworthiness. Businesses that prioritize long-term trust over short-term sales will always have a competitive advantage.

2.2 Emotional Triggers and the Science of Customer Loyalty

While logical factors like pricing and product features play a role in customer decisions, emotions often drive the final choice. People do not just buy products; they buy feelings—the feeling of security, excitement, belonging, or achievement. Businesses that understand this psychological reality can create marketing, messaging, and customer experiences that resonate deeply and forge strong emotional connections.

One of the most powerful emotional triggers is belonging. Customers want to feel like they are part of something larger than themselves. This is why communities and brand loyalty programs work so well. Apple, for example, does not just sell smartphones; it sells an identity. Apple users feel like they are part of an exclusive community, which is why many remain fiercely loyal to the brand, despite the availability of cheaper alternatives. Similarly, brands like Nike use emotional storytelling, highlighting perseverance, victory, and personal growth to create strong bonds with their audience.

Another significant emotional trigger is nostalgia. Many brands successfully appeal to customers by tapping into childhood memories, past experiences, or sentimental attachments. Coca-Cola, for instance, frequently uses nostalgic advertising to reinforce its brand as a symbol of comfort and tradition. This emotional connection makes the product feel more meaningful than just a soft drink; it becomes part of a person's personal history.

The fear of missing out (FOMO) is another powerful emotional driver. Customers are more likely to take action when they believe they might lose an opportunity. This is why limited time offers, exclusive memberships, and product scarcity strategies are effective. When customers believe they must act quickly to avoid missing out, they are more inclined to make purchasing decisions.

Security and peace of mind are also strong emotional triggers, particularly in industries like insurance, banking, and healthcare. Customers want to feel reassured that they are making the right choice and that their needs will be taken care of. This is why businesses that focus on risk reduction, clear guarantees, and hassle-free policies tend to attract more trust and loyalty. A bank that emphasizes fraud protection and financial education, for example, creates a sense of security for its customers, making them more likely to stay loyal.

Empathy is another underestimated tool in fostering customer loyalty. When customers feel that a business truly understands their challenges and cares about their well-being, they are more likely to stay engaged. Companies that go the extra mile to show empathy, whether by offering flexible payment plans, personalized customer support, or listening attentively to concerns create a deep emotional connection with their audience.

Understanding emotional triggers allows businesses to craft experiences that not only meet practical needs but also satisfy psychological desires. A business that can evoke positive emotions, reduce customer stress, and create a sense of belonging will not only attract customers but also retain them for the long term.

Every interaction with a customer, whether online, in person, or through customer service—provides an opportunity to learn. Businesses that listen to customer feedback, analyze behavioral data, and engage in direct conversations will always have a better understanding of what their audience truly wants. This knowledge becomes the foundation for better marketing, stronger relationships, and long-term customer loyalty.

CHAPTER THREE

BUILDING AUTHENTIC RELATIONSHIPS WITH CUSTOMERS

In the modern business landscape, success is no longer just about offering the best product or the lowest price, it is about building relationships that go beyond mere transactions. Customers are not just looking for businesses to buy from; they are looking for brands they can connect with, trust, and remain loyal to overtime. Businesses that cultivate authentic relationships with their customers not only retain them longer but also benefit from word-of-mouth marketing, repeat purchases, and a brand reputation that sets them apart from competitors.

Authenticity is at the heart of relationship-building. Customers today are more informed, skeptical, and selective about the brands they support. They are drawn to businesses that are genuine, transparent, and human in their approach. A company that treats its customers like mere numbers in a sales funnel will struggle to create long-term loyalty, while a brand that listens, engages, and builds trust will form deeper bonds that transcend one-time purchases.

At its core, an authentic relationship with customers is built on mutual respect, clear communication, and shared values. Businesses that focus solely on selling risk losing engagement over time, while those that genuinely invest in their customers' well-being foster stronger, longer-lasting connections.

One of the most effective ways to build authentic relationships with customers is through personalization. Customers do not want to feel like just another entry in a database, they want to feel recognized and valued as individuals. Personalization is more than just addressing a customer by their name in an email; it is about understanding their needs, preferences, and behaviors and tailoring interactions accordingly.

Successful businesses invest in data-driven personalization, using insights from customer behavior to offer customized recommendations, targeted content, and relevant offers. This is why e-commerce platforms like Amazon and streaming services like Netflix thrive, they analyze user data to provide personalized recommendations that make customers feel understood. When customers see that a brand remembers their preferences and anticipates their needs, they develop a deeper sense of connection and loyalty.

Personalization is also key in customer service. A company that remembers a customer's past interactions and provides a seamless, tailored experience will always stand out. Whether it is a restaurant remembering a regular customer's favorite dish or an online retailer sending special discounts based on past purchases, small personal touches create a big impact.

However, businesses must strike a balance, customers appreciate personalization, but they also value privacy. Personalization should be done in a way that enhances the experience without feeling intrusive. Companies that use data responsibly and transparently will earn more trust than those that collect information without clear consent.

Trust is the foundation of any authentic relationship, and trust is built on transparency. Customers appreciate brands that are honest, open, and clear in their communication. In contrast, businesses that make misleading claims, hide information, or manipulate customer perceptions will eventually lose credibility.

Transparency applies to various aspects of a business, from pricing and policies to marketing and customer service. A brand that clearly communicates what it offers, how it operates, and what customers can expect will always have an advantage over those that use deception or vague messaging.

A great example of transparency is companies that openly admit mistakes and take responsibility for them. Many businesses try to cover issues or shift blame when things go wrong, but customers appreciate brands that acknowledge their faults and work toward solutions. A company that says, "We made a mistake, and here's what we're doing to fix it," earns far more trust than one that ignores complaints or offers empty excuses.

Transparency is also crucial in handling customer feedback. Businesses that encourage open communication and actively listen to customer concerns build stronger relationships. Customers want to feel heard, and when they see that a company takes their opinions seriously, they become more engaged and invested in the brand's success.

Another key aspect of transparency is authentic storytelling. Many businesses try to craft a perfect image, but customers resonate more with brands that share real, relatable stories. Whether it is the origin of the company, the challenges faced along the way, or the impact the business hopes to make, authentic storytelling builds emotional connections that foster long-term loyalty.

A business that only interacts with customers when making a sale is unlikely to build lasting relationships. Customers appreciate brands that engage with them in meaningful, non-transactional ways. This means providing value beyond just selling a product, whether through educational content, community-building, or support initiatives.

Brands that create content that educates, entertains, or inspires their audience become more than just sellers, they become trusted sources of knowledge and value. A skincare brand that shares skincare tips, a financial institution that provides money management advice, or a fitness brand that offers free workout guides all build stronger relationships with their customers by being helpful rather than just promotional.

Community-building is another powerful strategy for deepening customer relationships. Brands that create forums, groups, or loyalty programs allow customers to connect not just with the business but with each other. These communities become spaces where people share experiences, ask for advice, and engage in meaningful discussions. A strong customer community reinforces loyalty, as members feel a sense of belonging and association with the brand.

A great example is Nike's running clubs by creating a space where customers can connect over a shared passion for fitness, Nike is not just selling shoes; it is fostering a lifestyle and an emotional connection with its audience.

Beyond engagement, businesses that support social causes or corporate responsibility initiatives also create deeper connections with their audience. Customers today are more likely to support brands that align with their values and contribute positively to society. Companies that take a stand on sustainability, ethical sourcing, or community development earn respect and loyalty from customers who care about these issues.

Building authentic relationships with customers is not just about increasing sales, it creates long-term business stability and growth. Customers who feel emotionally connected to a brand are more likely to remain loyal, recommend the brand to others, and defend it even in challenging times.

Customer advocacy is one of the biggest advantages of authentic relationships. A satisfied customer might make repeat purchases, but a loyal customer becomes an advocate, spreading positive word-of-mouth and bringing in new customers organically. Businesses that focus on relationship-building do not have to rely as heavily on expensive advertising, their customers become their best marketers.

Another major benefit is resilience during downturns or crises. Businesses that have strong relationships with their customers find that their audience is more forgiving and understanding when challenges arise. A company that has consistently provided great value and transparency will find that its customers are willing to stick with it even when prices increase, supply chain issues arise, or unexpected difficulties occur.

Furthermore, strong customer relationships lead to better feedback loops. When customers feel valued and connected to a brand, they are more likely to provide honest feedback that helps the business improve. This creates a cycle where the company continuously refines its offerings, leading to even greater customer satisfaction.

At the heart of every successful business is a deep commitment to fostering real connections with customers. Building authentic relationships requires personalization, transparency, meaningful engagement, and a focus on long-term value rather than short-term sales. Businesses that understand their customers, communicate openly, and create experiences that go beyond transactions will always stand out in a crowded market.

Building authentic relationships is about going beyond transactions, it is about cultivating trust, consistency, and emotional depth that transforms one-time buyers into lifelong supporters. Yet, many businesses struggle with maintaining authenticity in a time when marketing has become saturated with automation, AI-driven interactions, and mass communication. The brands that succeed are the ones that find ways to balance efficiency with a human touch, personalization with privacy, and innovation with authenticity.

Customer relationships are not just built on convenience or necessity, they are built on emotional attachment. Some brands become part of people's identities, and customers feel a sense of personal investment in their continued success. This is why Apple users fiercely defend the brand, why Nike customers feel inspired by its message of perseverance, and why luxury brands like Louis Vuitton and Rolex evoke a sense of status and exclusivity.

One of the biggest drivers of customer attachment is self-identity. People align themselves with brands that reflect their own values, aspirations, and lifestyles. A customer who prides themselves on environmental consciousness, for example, is more likely to support brands that promote sustainability. A tech enthusiast who values cutting-edge innovation will naturally gravitate toward brands that embody futuristic thinking.

Another factor that influences brand attachment is emotional resonance. Customers feel a stronger bond with brands that evoke positive emotions whether it is nostalgia, excitement, or a sense of community. This is why companies that tell compelling brand stories often have deeper customer relationships than those that focus solely on promotions. A brand that weaves itself into the emotional fabric of its customers' lives creates a powerful, lasting connection.

Take, for example, Coca-Cola's advertising strategy. Instead of simply promoting a carbonated beverage, the brand consistently associates itself with themes of happiness, togetherness, and shared moments. This emotional positioning makes customers feel something more than just thirst, it makes them feel connected to a larger, universal experience.

Businesses that understand how customer psychology influences brand loyalty can craft marketing and engagement strategies that go beyond rational decision-making and tap into emotional and subconscious motivations.

3.1 Restoring and Rebuilding Relationships After Mistakes

Even the best brands make mistakes. A delayed shipment, a faulty product, an unexpected price increase, or a customer service misstep can damage trust. However, what separates great businesses from average ones is how they respond when things go wrong. The way a company handles mistakes can either reinforce customer loyalty or drive customers away for good.

The first step in restoring a damaged customer relationship is acknowledgment. Many businesses make the error of avoiding responsibility, offering generic apologies, or trying to shift blame.

However, customers appreciate honesty and accountability. A sincere statement such as, "We made a mistake, and we take full responsibility for it," can go a long way in rebuilding trust.

Beyond words, businesses must take corrective action. If a product is defective, offer a replacement or refund immediately. If a customer has had a poor experience, provide a meaningful gesture to make up for it, whether that is a discount, a personalized apology, or a priority service upgrade. The goal should not just be to fix the issue but to exceed expectations in how it is resolved.

Timing also plays a critical role in damage control. The faster a business responds to a problem, the better the chances of salvaging the relationship. In today's digital age, where complaints can spread rapidly on social media, speed is crucial. A delayed response can give customers the impression that the company does not care.

Some of the most successful businesses have turned public relations crises into opportunities for stronger customer relationships by handling situations with transparency and proactive solutions. One example is JetBlue, an airline that suffered major delays during a winter storm in 2007. Instead of ignoring the backlash, JetBlue issued a sincere public apology, introduced a new "Passenger Bill of Rights," and compensated affected customers. The response not only restored customer trust but also positioned JetBlue as a brand that genuinely values its passengers.

Another great example is how Domino's Pizza transformed its reputation. After facing widespread criticism about the taste and quality of its pizza, the company launched an honest marketing campaign acknowledging the negative feedback. Instead of making excuses, Domino's openly admitted its shortcomings and committed to improving its recipe. The campaign was a massive success, and the brand saw a major turnaround in customer perception and sales. Businesses that view mistakes as opportunities to showcase accountability, integrity, and responsiveness often emerge with stronger customer relationships than before.

3.2 The Hidden Value of Surprise and Delight in Customer Relationships

A strong business-customer relationship is built on trust and consistency, but what truly deepens customer loyalty is the element of unexpected delight. When a business goes beyond the expected and surprises customers with small, meaningful gestures, it creates a memorable emotional experience that keeps customers coming back.

Surprise and delight can come in many forms, personalized thank-you notes, exclusive rewards, birthday discounts, free upgrades, or even small, unexpected gifts. These unexpected acts of generosity make customers feel appreciated and valued.

One example of this is Zappos, the online shoe retailer known for its legendary customer service. The company has been known to upgrade shipping for customers at no extra cost, deliver unexpected gifts, and even send flowers to customers going through tough times. This kind of personalized attention turns customers into lifelong fans.

Another example is Ritz-Carlton hotels, where staff are trained to go above and beyond to create unique customer experiences. There are countless stories of employees noticing small details like a guest's favorite drink or preference for extra pillows and proactively making their stay more comfortable without being asked. These little touches make guests feel more than just paying customers, they feel genuinely cared for.

Surprise and delight also play a role in customer retention strategies. Companies that reward long-term customers with unexpected perks, early access to new products, or VIP treatment create a sense of exclusivity that strengthens loyalty. What makes surprise and delight so powerful is that it is not expected. Customers anticipate standard service, but when a brand exceeds those expectations in an unexpected way, it creates an emotional high that strengthens attachment to the brand.

At its heart, customer relationship-building is about making people feel seen, valued, and connected. It is about creating a brand that does not just sell but resonates with its audience. Businesses that take the time to understand customer psychology, repair broken trust effectively, and add moments of unexpected delight will always have an advantage over those that focus solely on transactions.

Authenticity, empathy, and engagement are not optional in today's business world, they are essential pillars of lasting customer loyalty. Customers do not just want products and services; they want experiences, relationships, and brands that align with their identity and values.

CHAPTER FOUR

THE ART OF EXCEEDING CUSTOMER EXPECTATIONS

Meeting customer expectations is no longer enough in today's business landscape. With more choices available than ever before, customers gravitate toward brands that don't just deliver what they promised, but go beyond expectations in ways that surprise, delight, and create lasting impressions. The brands that truly stand out are those that consistently overdeliver, anticipate needs, and craft extraordinary experiences that customers can't forget.

Exceeding expectations is not about grand gestures or expensive perks, it's about understanding what customers value most and finding ways to enhance their experience in meaningful ways. Businesses that master this art build a strong foundation of trust, loyalty, and positive word-of-mouth, making it easier to retain customers and attract new ones effortlessly.

The key to exceeding expectations lies in proactive service, attention to detail, and a commitment to continuous improvement. Companies that go beyond the ordinary set themselves apart in an era where mediocrity is common. But how exactly do businesses achieve this level of excellence?

Customers always have a baseline expectation when they engage with a business. This expectation is shaped by a variety of factors, including past experiences, competitor offerings, advertising, and personal assumptions. When a business simply meets these expectations, the experience is seen as satisfactory but nothing more. However, when a business surpasses these expectations, it creates a memorable, standout moment that strengthens the customer's connection to the brand.

The expectation gap occurs when customers receive an experience that is either significantly better or significantly worse than what they anticipated. If the experience is worse, disappointment and frustration set in. If the experience is better, customers feel valued and are more likely to remain loyal. The goal of every business should be to identify gaps between what customers expect and what they receive, and then strategically close that gap by consistently overdelivering.

One of the simplest ways to exceed expectations is through speed and efficiency. Customers are used to businesses that take time to process requests, respond to inquiries, and resolve issues. When a company dramatically improves the speed of its service whether through faster delivery, quicker response times, or seamless transactions, customers take notice. A restaurant that delivers food in 20 minutes instead of the expected 45, or a support team that resolves issues in minutes instead of hours, creates a positive shock that leaves a lasting impact.

Another way to close the expectation gap is by offering unexpected extras. These can be small but meaningful gestures that go beyond what customers paid for or expected. This could be something as simple as a handwritten thank-you note in an online order, a complimentary dessert at a restaurant, or an extended warranty on a product at no additional cost. These "little surprises" make customers feel valued and appreciated, turning an ordinary experience into an exceptional one.

One of the hallmarks of businesses that exceed expectations is anticipation, the ability to foresee potential customer needs or problems before they arise and addressing them proactively. Instead of waiting for customers to express frustration or dissatisfaction, exceptional businesses take a proactive approach, ensuring that problems are solved before they even become an issue.

A great example of this is automated reminders and proactive communication. Banks that remind customers about upcoming payments before they incur late fees, airlines that notify travelers of flight delays well in advance, or online retailers that provide real-time tracking and proactive updates all show a commitment to reducing friction and increasing convenience. These small, proactive actions prevent frustration and enhance trust.

Anticipation also extends to personalized recommendations and guidance. Businesses that understand customer preferences can provide tailored suggestions that make customers feel like the brand truly understands them. Streaming services like Netflix and Spotify, for instance, go beyond providing entertainment, they anticipate what users might enjoy next based on their behavior, making discovery effortless and enjoyable. Similarly, a skincare brand that follows up with personalized product recommendations based on a customer's past purchases is not just selling, it is enhancing the customer's journey.

Exceeding expectations doesn't always require grand gestures often, it's the small details that leave the biggest impressions. Customers notice when businesses pay attention to the little things that matter most to them, and these moments can define their overall experience with the brand.

One example is packaging and presentation. A beautifully packaged product, an elegantly designed invoice, or a thoughtfully arranged store layout all contribute to how customers perceive value. Apple, for example, is famous for its sleek, carefully designed packaging that makes opening a new device feel like an experience in itself. This attention to detail reinforces the brand's identity as premium and thoughtful.

Customer service interactions also provide countless opportunities to exceed expectations. A hotel receptionist who remembers a guest's name and favorite drink, a call center agent who follows up personally after resolving an issue, or a retail employee who goes out of their way to help a customer find the perfect product all create meaningful, memorable moments that set businesses apart.

Even the tone and personality of a brand's communication can make a difference. A friendly, conversational email instead of a generic automated response, or a playful social media reply that makes a customer smile, can turn a standard interaction into something delightful.

For a business to consistently exceed customer expectations, the mindset of going the extra mile must be embedded in its culture. It cannot just be a marketing strategy or a customer service department initiative, it must be a company-wide philosophy that every team member embraces.

This starts with leadership. Business leaders must set the tone by prioritizing excellence, valuing customer experience, and rewarding employees who go above and beyond. When employees see that delivering outstanding service is appreciated and encouraged, they become more motivated to take the initiative and create exceptional experiences for customers.

Empowering employees to make decisions also plays a crucial role. When frontline staff have the autonomy to solve customer issues creatively, they can provide faster, more personalized solutions instead of relying on rigid policies. Companies like Ritz-Carlton, for instance, empower their employees to spend up to $2,000 per guest per day to resolve customer concerns without needing management approval.

This level of empowerment allows staff to act quickly and provide meaningful resolutions that exceed expectations.

Training and continuous learning also contribute to a culture of excellence. Businesses that invest in ongoing training for employees, teaching them not just the mechanics of their roles but the art of customer delight will naturally outperform competitors who see customer service as a secondary function. Employees who are trained to think like customers, anticipate needs, and create memorable experiences become invaluable assets to the company.

Businesses that consistently exceed expectations enjoy a range of benefits that go beyond immediate customer satisfaction. Customer loyalty, brand reputation, and increased word-of-mouth referrals all come naturally to companies that prioritize excellence.

Satisfied customers are more likely to become repeat buyers, and loyal customers are significantly more valuable than new customers. Studies show that increasing customer retention by just 5% can boost profits by 25% to 95%. Businesses that focus on overdelivering not only keep their customers longer but also spend less on acquiring new ones, as happy customers become organic brand advocates.

Additionally, customers who have positive, surprising experiences with a brand are more likely to share their stories. Whether through online reviews, social media, or personal recommendations, a customer who is genuinely delighted will spread the word and no marketing campaign is more powerful than genuine, unpaid endorsements from real customers.

Ultimately, exceeding expectations is not just about making customers happy, it is about making them feel valued, understood, and excited to return. Businesses that integrate this philosophy into their core operations will create a legacy of excellence, setting themselves apart as brands that customers can't help but love.

Customers remember exceptional experiences, but they also remember disappointments. The difference between a business that thrives and one that merely survives is the ability to consistently surpass expectations in ways that create lasting emotional connections. In an era where consumers have endless choices, businesses that go beyond the standard level of service establish a deep sense of trust and loyalty that competitors struggle to replicate.

Exceeding expectations does not mean making grand, unsustainable gestures. It is about building a business culture that values small, meaningful acts of kindness, responsiveness, and personalization. When customers feel that a business understands them, values their time, and anticipates their needs, they are more likely to remain loyal and even become advocates for the brand. The real secret to exceeding expectations lies in making every interaction with a customer feel effortless, thoughtful, and intentional.

Customers today are not just comparing businesses within the same industry; they are comparing experiences across industries. A customer who enjoys a seamless, personalized experience when shopping on an e-commerce site will expect the same level of efficiency when dealing with their bank or healthcare provider. This shift in consumer behavior means that businesses can no longer afford to meet only the basic requirements of a good service, they must be constantly raising the bar.

One of the most underestimated ways to exceed expectations is by eliminating friction. Customers often tolerate inconveniences because they have become used to them, but when a business proactively removes unnecessary steps, speeds up a process, or simplifies interactions, it stands out. A company that allows customers to return items without hassle, book appointments in seconds, or access support without long waiting times instantly becomes more valuable in the customer's eyes. Businesses that identify common pain points and proactively resolve them before customers even have to ask are remembered as problem solvers rather than service providers.

Going beyond expectations also requires businesses to be emotionally intelligent. Customers often approach businesses with a need, sometimes urgent, sometimes complex. The ability to recognize emotions in customer interactions and respond with warmth, reassurance, and care creates a level of trust that purely transactional businesses fail to achieve. A customer who receives a thoughtful follow-up after making a complaint, or a sincere apology rather than a scripted response, feels heard and respected. Businesses that make emotional intelligence a priority train their teams to see customers not as tasks to be completed but as people to be understood.

Businesses that truly exceed expectations also understand the power of memorable touchpoints. These are the moments in the customer journey where a brand has an opportunity to make an impression that lingers. Whether it is the unboxing experience of a new product, a follow-up email that feels personal rather than automated, or a loyalty program that genuinely rewards engagement, these touchpoints create emotional imprints that lead to long-term customer commitment.

Surprise is another key element in exceeding expectations. When customers receive unexpected value, they feel a strong emotional connection to a brand. This could be an unannounced upgrade, a handwritten thank-you note, a faster-than-expected delivery, or even a simple gesture like offering complimentary refreshments at a store. These surprises do not have to be extravagant; they just have to be meaningful.

One of the biggest misconceptions in business is that exceeding expectations requires extra resources or heavy financial investments. In reality, it is not about spending more; it is about thinking differently. A brand that takes the time to remember a returning customer's preferences, resolve an issue proactively, or offer personalized recommendations without being asked creates a feeling of being valued and understood without incurring additional costs.

Exceeding expectations does not only apply to customer service, it extends to product quality, user experience, and business ethics. A company that consistently delivers reliable, high-quality products without defects is already surpassing many expectations. A software company that continuously updates its platform with useful features based on customer feedback shows attentiveness that competitors may not. A business that operates with transparency and strong ethical values, ensuring fair pricing and sustainable practices, earns the admiration and trust of socially conscious consumers.

Customer expectations are dynamic, and what is considered extraordinary today may become the standard tomorrow. This is why businesses must continuously innovate in how they surprise and delight customers. A brand that rests on past achievements without looking for new ways to improve will eventually be overtaken by competitors who are always optimizing, refining, and adapting to evolving customer needs.

Exceeding expectations also means empowering customers. Businesses that give customers more control, whether through self-service options, personalized account management, or loyalty rewards that let them choose their perks, create a sense of partnership rather than dependency. Customers feel more satisfied when they are not just passive recipients of a service but active participants in shaping their own experiences.

A key part of overdelivering is knowing when and how to recover from service failures gracefully. Even the most well-run businesses will experience issues, orders may get delayed, mistakes may happen, or customers may feel unsatisfied with a particular interaction. The way a business handles these moments defines its reputation. A business that takes accountability, provides a genuine apology, and compensates customers fairly turns a potential disaster into an opportunity to reinforce trust. Some of the most loyal customers are those who have experienced a problem and seen firsthand how well a company resolves it.

What sets truly exceptional brands apart is their commitment to consistency in exceeding expectations. It is not enough to surprise a customer once, great businesses make overdelivering a standard practice rather than an occasional marketing tactic. The goal is to create a brand identity where customers come to expect excellence, and that expectation is met every single time.

Exceeding expectations should not be limited to a company's interactions with customers, it should also be applied internally. Companies that create an internal culture of excellence where employees feel valued, empowered, and inspired to go beyond the basic requirements of their roles, naturally deliver better service. Happy, motivated employees take pride in delighting customers, and their enthusiasm translates into superior customer experiences.

The businesses that succeed long-term are those that treat exceeding expectations as a philosophy rather than a strategy. They recognize that customers are not obligated to stay loyal, they stay because they feel appreciated, understood, and continuously surprised by how much value they receive.

A brand that goes beyond expectations does not just retain customers, it creates ambassadors who share their exceptional experiences with others. Word-of-mouth recommendations from customers who have been truly impressed carry far more weight than any marketing campaign. The more a business exceeds expectations, the more its customers become its most powerful advocates, freely promoting the brand because they genuinely believe in it.

Customers today have access to a limitless number of choices, which means businesses must do more than just deliver a service or product, they must create experiences that stand out. Exceeding expectations is not about chance; it is about being intentional, strategic, and committed to delighting customers at every touchpoint. While we have explored the importance of surprise, emotional intelligence, and consistency, there are deeper layers to customer satisfaction that many businesses overlook. Going beyond expectations also involves **empowering customers**, understanding the role of **social validation**, and recognizing that exceptional experiences extend beyond individual transactions.

4.1 Empowering Customers to Elevate Their Own Experience

One of the most overlooked ways to exceed expectations is by giving customers more control over their interactions with a business. Empowering customers does not mean simply providing more options, it means allowing them to customize their experience, make informed decisions, and feel a sense of ownership over their engagement with the brand.

Modern customers value autonomy. They appreciate it when a business gives them tools to personalize their experiences, whether it is through self-service portals, flexible subscription models, or customized product recommendations. Companies that exceed expectations do not just offer a one-size-fits-all solution; they let customers tailor their experience to fit their unique needs and preferences.

For example, streaming platforms like Netflix and Spotify allow users to curate their own content by providing personalized recommendations, custom playlists, and the ability to save favorites. Customers feel empowered because the platform learns from their behaviors and continuously refines their experience. This approach can be applied to virtually any business, whether it is an airline allowing customers to choose their seat and meal preferences in advance, a fashion retailer offering a virtual fitting room, or a bank enabling users to set their own transaction limits for security purposes.

Empowerment also comes from providing clear, transparent information that allows customers to make better decisions. Businesses that exceed expectations do not just offer a product or service; they educate customers on how to maximize their value. This is why companies that provide tutorials, guides, and customer communities where users can share tips often have higher satisfaction rates. A brand that invests in customer education creates a relationship based on trust and empowerment, ensuring that users feel confident in their choices.

Another way businesses can empower customers is by offering flexible engagement. Rigid policies and strict rules often frustrate customers, making them feel restricted rather than valued. Companies that introduce lenient return policies, pay-as-you-go pricing, or on-demand customer service allow customers to feel in control of their interactions. The more freedom a business gives customers to shape their journey, the more positive and memorable that experience becomes.

4.2 The Role of Social Proof in Exceeding Expectations

Customers do not just evaluate a business based on their personal experiences—they look to social proof to validate their perceptions. Social proof is a psychological phenomenon where people assume the actions of others reflect the correct behavior in a given situation. In the business world, it means that customer reviews, testimonials, and word-of-mouth recommendations significantly influence buying decisions.

A business that wants to exceed expectations must recognize that its reputation is not just built on what it delivers, but also on how customers share their experiences with others. Companies that actively encourage, highlight, and respond to customer feedback set themselves apart as brands that care about public perception and continuous improvement.

The most impactful form of social proof comes from real, authentic testimonials. Customers trust other customers more than they trust marketing messages. Businesses that showcase user-generated content whether it is unfiltered reviews, video testimonials, or customer case studies build stronger credibility than those that rely solely on self-promotion. Seeing a peer endorse a product or service feels far more reliable than reading a corporate sales pitch.

Exceeding expectations also means creating moments that customers want to talk about. The best word-of-mouth marketing happens organically when customers are so delighted by an experience that they feel compelled to share it. Businesses that craft moments of unexpected joy, whether it is a hotel leaving a handwritten note for a guest, a restaurant sending complimentary desserts, or a brand surprising loyal customers with exclusive perks create stories that get retold, reinforcing positive perceptions.

Social validation is also important in building a sense of community around a brand. Customers are more likely to engage deeply with businesses that foster a loyal, interactive customer base. This is why brands that build forums, social media groups, and loyalty programs that connect customers with one another often see higher levels of brand engagement. A customer who feels like they are part of a larger movement or shared experience is far more likely to remain loyal.

Another critical aspect of social proof is responsiveness to public feedback. Businesses that take the time to engage with customer reviews, acknowledge concerns, and publicly resolve issues demonstrate accountability and a commitment to excellence. Customers pay attention to how businesses respond to criticism, and companies that handle negative feedback with grace and a genuine willingness to improve often gain more trust than those that ignore or delete complaints.

In today's digital landscape, social validation plays an enormous role in how customers perceive value. A brand that exceeds expectations does not just focus on individual transactions; it ensures that every customer becomes a vocal advocate for the experience they received.

The art of exceeding expectations is not a one-time effort; it is a philosophy that must be woven into the very fabric of a business. It is about creating an environment where every customer interaction, no matter how small, is treated as an opportunity to surprise, delight, and build lasting relationships.

Businesses that master this art do not just deliver products or services; they curate experiences that customers want to return to. They remove barriers, anticipate needs, and ensure that every detail of the customer journey is designed with thoughtfulness.

Exceeding expectations is not just about making customers happy in the moment, it is about creating an emotional impact that turns them into lifelong advocates. The brands that recognize this, and commit to going beyond the expected, are the ones that thrive in today's hyper-competitive market.

CHAPTER FIVE

TRUST AS A COMPETITIVE ADVANTAGE

Trust is the foundation of every successful business relationship. Customers may be attracted to a brand because of its marketing, pricing, or product quality, but what keeps them coming back is trust. In today's marketplace, where competition is fierce and consumer skepticism is at an all-time high, businesses that establish and maintain trust gain a significant advantage over those that focus solely on transactions. Trust is not just about honesty; it is about reliability, consistency, transparency, and genuine customer care.

Consumers today have access to more information than ever before. They read reviews, compare brands, and seek out authentic customer experiences before making a purchase. If they sense even the slightest dishonesty, hidden agenda, or lack of reliability, they will move on to a competitor. Businesses that understand this reality focus not only on delivering value but also on cultivating deep, long-term relationships built on credibility and dependability.

Trust is fragile. It takes time to build but can be destroyed in an instant. A single negative experience, an unfulfilled promise, or a misleading claim can cause a loyal customer to walk away forever. This is why companies that prioritize trust do not make promises they cannot keep, do not exaggerate their offerings, and do not take customer loyalty for granted.

The brands that command the most trust are those that remain consistent in their messaging, service, and ethical practices. Customers feel more secure when they know what to expect and when a business delivers on its commitments every time. A company that constantly changes policies, increases prices without explanation, or provides inconsistent service creates uncertainty, which erodes trust over time.

Trust is also closely tied to openness and transparency. Customers appreciate businesses that are clear about their pricing, policies, and limitations. When a company openly communicates why certain decisions are made, whether it is a price adjustment, a product recall, or a delay in service, customers are more likely to remain loyal because they feel respected and valued. Businesses that hide behind fine print, misleading advertisements, or vague terms inevitably lose credibility.

A major aspect of building trust is being proactive about customer concerns. The best businesses do not wait for complaints to escalate before taking action, they anticipate potential issues and address them before they become problems. Whether it provides clear return policies, offering warranties, or being upfront about potential risks, proactive trust-building makes customers feel secure in their decision to support a brand.

One of the most powerful ways businesses earn trust is through social proof. Customers are far more likely to believe what other customers say about a brand than what the brand says about itself. Positive reviews, testimonials, case studies, and word-of-mouth recommendations all reinforce a company's credibility. A business that actively encourages and showcases customer feedback, rather than hiding from it, signals confidence in its offerings.

Another crucial element of trust is authenticity. Customers today can spot insincerity from a mile away. Businesses that try too hard to be something they are not, whether through forced branding, scripted interactions, or exaggerated claims fail to connect on a deeper level. The most trusted brands are those that stay true to their identity, values, and mission. They communicate with genuine personality, acknowledge their mistakes, and constantly seek to improve without pretending to be perfect.

Responsiveness is another key driver of trust. Customers want to feel heard and valued. When they reach out to a company with questions, concerns, or feedback, the speed and quality of the response determine how much they trust the brand. A business that takes days to respond to inquiries or provides generic, unhelpful replies will struggle to earn long-term loyalty. On the other hand, a business that acknowledges and addresses customer concerns promptly, whether through social media, live chat, or personal outreach strengthens its reputation as a reliable brand.

Ethical business practices also play a huge role in trust-building. Companies that treat employees well, engage in sustainable practices, and operate with integrity earn not only customer trust but also public goodwill. Consumers today are more conscious than ever about the ethical implications of their purchases. Businesses that exploit workers, damage the environment, or engage in unethical financial practices may see short-term gains but will ultimately suffer long-term consequences.

Trust is also about admitting mistakes and making things right. No business is perfect, and customers do not expect perfection. What they do expect is accountability. When a company makes a mistake, how it handles the situation determines whether customers will forgive or walk away. Brands that acknowledge errors, offer sincere apologies, and take concrete steps to fix the issue often come out stronger than before. In many cases, how a company responds to failure can actually increase customer loyalty.

Beyond service and transparency, trust is also built through product reliability. A company that consistently delivers high-quality products that function as promised will naturally earn customer confidence. This is why trusted brands often offer warranties, guarantees, and refund policies, they stand behind their products and services because they know they are delivering genuine value.

The businesses that successfully leverage trust as a competitive advantage do not just retain customers, they create passionate brand advocates. Customers who trust a brand do not just buy from it; they defend it, recommend it, and remain loyal even in the face of competition. Trust reduces price sensitivity, meaning customers are often willing to pay more for a brand they believe in, even when cheaper alternatives exist.

Trust is not something that can be built overnight, nor is it something that can be taken for granted. It requires ongoing commitment, ethical decision-making, and a relentless focus on customer well-being. The companies that recognize this and embed trust into every aspect of their operations will not only survive in today's crowded marketplace but will thrive for decades to come.

Trust is not just a business strategy; it is the foundation of sustainable growth and long-term success. In a world where customers have countless choices and instant access to information, trust is what differentiates a brand from its competitors. Businesses that cultivate trust gain more than just loyal customers; they gain **brand advocates** who actively promote their products, defend their reputation, and remain committed even when competitors offer lower prices or new innovations. Trust is a currency that businesses must continuously invest in, and those that do will see returns in customer retention, reputation, and long-term profitability.

Customers do not extend trust easily, nor do they give it unconditionally. Trust is earned through consistency, transparency, reliability, and ethical behavior. A single broken promise, a misleading claim, or a poor customer service experience can undo years of effort in building trust. This is why businesses that prioritize trust must integrate it into every aspect of their operations from leadership and communication to product quality and customer interactions. Trust cannot be treated as an afterthought; it must be embedded into the company culture, values, and brand promise.

One of the primary reasons trusts is a competitive advantage because it reduces uncertainty for customers. In a market filled with options, consumers naturally gravitate toward brands they trust because it minimizes their risk. A customer who trusts a brand does not have to second-guess whether the product will work, whether the service will be reliable, or whether their personal information will be handled responsibly. Trust simplifies decision-making and strengthens the emotional bond between the customer and the business.

Businesses that understand the power of trust actively demonstrate integrity in their actions. They do not just claim to be trustworthy; they prove it through their behavior. This is why some of the most respected brands in the world are those that stand by their commitments, even when it is inconvenient or costly. Companies that voluntarily recall defective products, issue refunds without hassle, or take responsibility for mistakes build a level of trust that competitors struggle to match.

Trust is closely tied to fairness and ethical business practices. Customers trust companies that treat their employees well, use sustainable practices, and engage in fair pricing. Brands that are caught exploiting workers, engaging in deceptive advertising, or prioritizing profits over people inevitably lose credibility. In contrast, businesses that operate with transparency and ethical integrity attract not only loyal customers but also top talent who want to work for companies they believe in.

Another key element of trust is predictability. Customers appreciate brands that are reliable and consistent in their offerings. If a company provides high-quality products and excellent service today but fails to do so tomorrow, trust is eroded. Businesses that maintain the same level of excellence over time create a sense of security that keeps customers coming back. This is why some brands, even after decades in business, continue to dominate their industries because they have built a reputation for unwavering reliability.

A major factor that influences trust is how a company handles customer feedback and complaints. Every business will face dissatisfied customers at some point, but how they respond to these moments defines their trustworthiness. Brands that ignore complaints, provide generic responses, or try to silence criticism lose credibility. On the other hand, businesses that take customer concerns seriously address them openly, and make meaningful changes based on feedback show commitment to continuous improvement. A company that listens to its customers and acts on their input reinforces the idea that customer satisfaction is truly a priority.

In today's digital landscape, trust is also built through social proof and third-party validation. Customers are more likely to believe real user experiences than marketing claims. This is why businesses that encourage customer reviews, showcase testimonials, and engage with their audience on social media build stronger credibility. A brand that is consistently praised by customers is far more trustworthy than one that relies solely on self-promotion. Additionally, businesses that have been recognized by independent review sites, industry awards, or media outlets gain even more credibility, as these endorsements act as external verification of their reliability.

Trust is also reinforced by a company's willingness to be transparent about its operations, policies, and challenges. Businesses that try to hide information or mislead customers will eventually be exposed, and the damage to their reputation can be irreversible. In contrast, companies that openly communicate about changes in pricing, product availability, or internal challenges earn respect. Customers appreciate honesty, even when the news is not ideal. A company that says, "We're experiencing delays due to supply chain issues, but here's what we're doing to fix it," builds more trust than one that stays silent and leaves customers guessing.

Another critical aspect of trust is security and data protection. In an era where cybersecurity threats and data breaches are common, customers are more cautious about sharing personal information. Businesses that take privacy seriously, invest in secure systems, and communicate how they protect customer data build a strong foundation of trust. Brands that misuse customer information, sell data without consent, or fail to safeguard personal details will quickly lose credibility and face serious consequences.

Trust is not only important in customer relationships but also in business partnerships. Companies that are known for their ethical dealings, fair negotiations, and dependable commitments attract better partnerships and collaborations. Vendors, suppliers, and investors prefer working with brands that have a solid reputation because they know they can rely on them. This expands the business opportunities and strengthens its position in the market.

The long-term benefits of trust cannot be overstated. Trust reduces customer churn, increases customer lifetime value, and makes customers less price sensitive. A customer who trusts a brand is less likely to switch to a competitor, even if that competitor offers a cheaper alternative. This is because trust is not just about cost, it is about security, reliability, and peace of mind.

Building trust is not a one-time effort; it is an ongoing commitment. Businesses that focus on consistent quality, open communication, ethical decision-making, and a genuine customer-first approach will always have a competitive advantage. Trust is not just what keeps customers coming back, it is what makes them feel connected to a brand, proud to support it, and willing to recommend it to others.

Trust is built over time, but it can be lost in an instant. A single deceptive practice, poor product experience, or lack of accountability can erode years of goodwill. This is why companies that wish to remain competitive must view trust as an active, ongoing commitment rather than a passive expectation. Consumers today demand more than just good service; they seek authenticity, ethical responsibility, and a commitment to excellence.

5.1 The Role of Consistency in Trust-Building

One of the most fundamental yet overlooked aspects of trust-building is consistency. Customers trust brands that deliver the same quality of experience every time they interact. A business that is unpredictable in service, pricing, or product quality creates uncertainty, which makes customers hesitant to remain loyal.

Consistency does not mean rigid uniformity; it means ensuring that every customer interaction aligns with the company's core values and brand promise. Whether a customer engages with a brand online, in-store, or through customer service, the experience should feel familiar and reassuring. When businesses deliver consistently great service, they reinforce reliability and dependability, both of which are essential to trust.

A prime example of consistency in action is fast-food chains like McDonald's and Starbucks. No matter where customers visit, they expect a certain level of quality and service, and these brands deliver. This predictability builds confidence, making customers less likely to switch to a competitor.

Another aspect of consistency is how businesses handle customer concerns and disputes. Customers pay close attention to how a company responds when things go wrong. A brand that consistently resolves issues fairly, apologizes sincerely, and offers meaningful solutions will earn more trust than one that is inconsistent in its approach. A customer should not feel uncertain about whether they will be treated well, it should be a given.

Consistency also applies to brand messaging and values. A company that frequently changes its positioning, slogans, or values confuses customers. A brand that claims to care about sustainability but does not implement ethical sourcing practices will quickly lose trust. Trust is strengthened by alignment when a business's words match its actions, customers feel reassured that the company is genuine.

5.2 Trust as a Buffer Against Competition and Market Fluctuations

One of the most powerful benefits of trust is that it acts as a protective shield against competition. In industries where multiple businesses offer similar products or services, trust becomes the ultimate differentiator. A brand that has consistently earned customer trust does not need to compete solely with price or features, it competes with emotional connection and reliability.

Customers are willing to pay a premium for brands they trust because trust reduces perceived risk. When consumers feel secure in their relationship with a business, they do not feel the need to constantly shop around for alternatives. This is why luxury brands, premium service providers, and industry leaders often charge higher prices, customers are not just buying a product; they are buying peace of mind.

Trust also makes businesses more resilient during market downturns. During economic uncertainty, customers become more cautious about where they spend their money. Brands with a strong trust foundation often retain customers even when spending slows down. Customers are more likely to remain loyal to a company that has consistently treated them well, rather than switching to a cheaper but less reliable alternative.

Moreover, trust creates a long-term competitive moat. Companies that invest in trust-building are not easily disrupted by new entrants in the market. While a competitor may enter with lower prices or aggressive marketing, they will struggle to win over loyal customers who already trust an established brand. Trust makes switching difficult not because customers cannot find alternatives, but because they do not want to take the risk of moving away from a company they know and rely on.

Another advantage of trust is that it amplifies customer advocacy. Loyal customers who trust a brand are more likely to recommend it to friends and family, leave positive reviews, and defend the brand in public discussions. This organic word-of-mouth marketing is far more valuable than paid advertising because it carries the weight of genuine customer experiences.

Businesses that wish to future-proof themselves should make trust a core pillar of their strategy. It should be seen not as a byproduct of good service but as a deliberate goal that influences decision-making, company culture, and long-term planning. Trust is what keeps customers returning, even when the market changes, technology evolves, or competitors attempt to disrupt the industry.

CHAPTER SIX

LEADERSHIP AND CUSTOMER LOYALTY

The role of leadership in cultivating customer loyalty cannot be overstated. Leaders set the tone for how a company values, prioritizes, and interacts with its customers. Their decisions, attitudes, and philosophies shape not only internal culture but also the overall customer experience. When leadership is customer-centric, it creates an organization that places loyalty at the heart of its operations. Leaders who truly understand the importance of customer loyalty go beyond viewing customers as mere revenue sources. Instead, they see them as long-term partners, recognizing that sustainable business success is built on repeat patronage, trust, and emotional connection.

Businesses that maintain strong customer loyalty are often led by individuals who embed customer satisfaction into their corporate vision. They do not simply delegate customer care to frontline employees but instead ensure that every department; marketing, sales, operations, product development, and even finance aligns with the goal of enhancing customer relationships. These leaders actively engage with customers, listen to their concerns, and make strategic decisions based on real customer insights rather than assumptions. Instead of focusing only on quarterly revenue goals, they look at customer retention metrics, satisfaction scores, and long-term engagement.

One of the most crucial traits of leaders who drive customer loyalty is their ability to instill a culture of service excellence. A company where leadership values customer happiness creates an environment where employees are motivated to go above and beyond for customers. Employees take their cues from management, if leaders treat customers as replaceable, so will their teams. However, when leaders demonstrate a genuine commitment to exceeding customer expectations, that mindset trickles down through the entire organization. Employees who feel empowered to take initiative in solving customer problems, making accommodations, and adding personal touches to interactions will naturally create more loyal customers.

The way leadership approaches employee satisfaction is also deeply connected to customer loyalty. Happy employees create happy customers. A company where leadership fosters a positive work culture, values employee contributions, and provides fair compensation and growth opportunities will naturally have a workforce that is more engaged, dedicated, and willing to deliver exceptional service. Conversely, a toxic work environment where employees feel undervalued and unmotivated will result in poor customer experiences. Customers can sense when employees are disengaged, and that lack of enthusiasm directly impacts their perception of the brand. A leader who understands this dynamic ensures that employees feel as valued as customers because they know that internal satisfaction translates into external excellence.

Beyond culture, leadership decisions around company policies, product development, and service innovation play a critical role in customer loyalty. Leaders who prioritize convenience, fairness, and transparency make it easier for customers to remain loyal. A company that frequently changes its pricing structures without clear communication, introduces hidden fees, or makes it difficult for customers to resolve issues creates frustration and erodes trust. Conversely, a business that offers simple, fair pricing, straightforward return policies, and accessible customer support demonstrates that it values long-term relationships over short-term gains. Customers notice when a company is designed to serve them rather than extracting as much value as possible from them.

Another key factor in leadership-driven customer loyalty is how a company handles mistakes and crises. No business is perfect, and even the most customer-focused companies will experience service failures, product recalls, or PR crises. What separates companies that retain loyal customers from those that lose them is how leadership responds in these moments. Businesses that acknowledge their mistakes, communicate transparently, and offer sincere solutions gain even greater trust from customers. Those that attempt to cover issues, shift blame, or provide dismissive responses often find themselves losing not only current customers but also future prospects as word of their handling of the situation spreads. A strong leader takes ownership of problems, views them as opportunities to demonstrate integrity, and works actively to make things right.

The role of trust in leadership also extends beyond direct customer interactions. It involves ethical business practices, corporate responsibility, and an unwavering commitment to delivering on promises. Customers today are more conscious than ever of where they spend their money. They want to support brands that align with their values, treat employees fairly, engage in sustainable practices, and operate with integrity. When leadership prioritizes these ethical considerations, they foster a level of customer loyalty that goes beyond transactions. Customers feel good about supporting businesses they trust and respect. This is why brands that commit to fair trade, environmental sustainability, and community development initiatives often enjoy a higher level of customer retention and advocacy.

Technology has also shifted the role of leadership in customer loyalty. Digital transformation has created more ways for companies to engage with customers, but it has also raised expectations. Leaders must ensure that their companies leverage technology to enhance customer experiences rather than create new frustrations. This means implementing seamless online interactions, providing personalized recommendations based on customer data, and using automation where it enhances convenience rather than replacing human connection. A business that automates everything at the expense of meaningful engagement risks alienating customers who still value human interaction. The best leaders find the balance between efficiency and personal touch, ensuring that customers feel both understood and valued in every interaction.

Loyalty also depends on a company's ability to evolve with its customers. Businesses that fail to adapt to changing customer needs eventually become irrelevant, no matter how strong their brand once was. Leadership must stay ahead of industry trends, anticipate shifts in consumer behavior, and proactively innovate. Companies that stagnate or resist change often see their most loyal customers outgrow them in favor of brands that better meet their evolving needs. Strong leaders recognize that customer loyalty is not about keeping things the same, it is about maintaining trust while continuously improving and adapting to serve customers better.

The long-term benefits of leadership-driven customer loyalty extend far beyond individual transactions. A business with a strong base of loyal customers enjoys more stability, better word-of-mouth marketing, and lower acquisition costs. Loyal customers act as brand ambassadors, freely recommending the business to their networks, which is far more powerful than any paid advertising campaign. Customer retention is also significantly more cost-effective than customer acquisition, and companies that prioritize keeping their existing customers satisfied ultimately spend less on marketing and sales efforts.

Leadership that fosters customer loyalty also creates a sense of belonging. Customers who feel a deep connection to a brand are not just repeat buyers, they become part of a larger community. Businesses that recognize this dynamic invest in relationship-building, personalized communication, and ongoing engagement strategies that make customers feel like insiders rather than outsiders. A leader who understands this ensures that customers are not just purchasing products or services but are becoming part of something meaningful.

Ultimately, leadership and customer loyalty are inseparable. A company's ability to retain customers is a direct reflection of its leadership's values, priorities, and long-term vision. Leaders who champion customer satisfaction as a core business objective create brands that stand the test of time. They build organizations where customers are not just numbers but valued relationships that deserve attention, care, and respect. Companies that integrate customer loyalty into their leadership philosophy do not just retain customers, they create lifelong advocates who support, defend, and promote the brand.

The strength of any company's customer loyalty is a direct reflection of its leadership. Every successful brand with a deeply loyal customer base has leaders who have deliberately shaped a company culture that values customer relationships over short-term gains. While businesses often focus on marketing tactics to build loyalty, the most sustainable form of customer retention comes from leadership that embeds trust, consistency, and value into every aspect of the business. Customers can sense when a company is run by leaders who genuinely care about them, and that care is what transforms ordinary buyers into lifelong supporters.

Great leadership in customer loyalty begins with a clear and compelling vision. Customers do not just remain loyal to companies because of the products or services they offer; they stay because they believe in the brand's mission, identity, and purpose. Leaders who cultivate strong loyalty are those who ensure that their company stands for something beyond profit. They create an emotional connection between the brand and its customers by clearly communicating why the company exists, what it values, and how it improves customers' lives. This vision should not just be a corporate statement, it should be embedded in every business decision, employee interaction, and customer touchpoint.

Consistency in leadership is another critical factor in maintaining customer loyalty. A company's ability to keep customers depends largely on how predictable and reliable its service is. Customers want to know that they can expect the same level of quality, responsiveness, and care every time they engage with a business. Leaders who enforce high standards in every department, ensuring that marketing, product development, and customer service all align with the company's promise, create a sense of stability that keeps customers coming back. A company that fluctuates in quality, changes its values based on trends, or fails to meet the expectations it sets for itself will inevitably lose trust, no matter how great its products are.

Empowering employees is one of the most overlooked aspects of leadership-driven customer loyalty. Leaders who recognize that employee satisfaction directly impacts customer satisfaction create workplaces where team members feel motivated to deliver outstanding experiences. Customers can tell when employees are engaged, enthusiastic, and empowered to solve problems rather than restricted by rigid policies and unnecessary bureaucracy. When leadership encourages employees to take ownership of customer relationships—whether by personalizing interactions, resolving issues efficiently, or simply making customers feel valued—loyalty grows naturally. This approach ensures that every customer touchpoint is infused with a sense of care and attentiveness that cannot be faked or scripted.

Trust is another pillar of leadership that influences customer loyalty. The most successful brands are those that customers trust implicitly, knowing that they will always act with integrity, honesty, and fairness. This trust is not built through advertising or promotional campaigns, it is built through years of consistently ethical decision-making and transparent communication. Leaders who make trust a core business priority ensure that their brands always deliver on promises, provide clear and honest information, and handle challenges in a way that respects the customer. They resist the temptation of short-term deception in favor of long-term credibility. Customers may forget discounts and special offers, but they never forget how a company made them feel, especially in moments when trust was put to the test.

Handling crises and mistakes with integrity is another defining trait of leaders who cultivate loyalty. No business is perfect, and even the best brands will face service failures, public relations setbacks, or operational challenges. What separates strong leaders from weak ones is how they respond to these moments. A company that issues a sincere apology, communicates openly with customers, and provides fair solutions reinforces its trustworthiness. Businesses that attempt to ignore problems, shift blame, or downplay legitimate concerns send a clear message to customers that their loyalty is not valued. In contrast, brands that handle crises with grace often find that customer loyalty actually increases because people respect and appreciate honesty.

Customer loyalty is also influenced by how much leaders prioritize innovation and adaptation. Businesses cannot afford to remain stagnant; they must constantly evolve to meet changing customer needs, technological advancements, and competitive pressures. Leaders who embrace innovation without compromising the trust and core values of their brand create companies that remain relevant for decades. This does not mean changing a company's identity to chase trends but rather adapting while staying true to what made the brand successful in the first place. Customers who see a business consistently improving and introducing valuable new offerings feel a sense of excitement and anticipation, which strengthens their connection to the brand.

One of the most powerful ways leadership drives customer loyalties is through personal engagement and accessibility. Customers feel more connected to brands where leadership is visible, approachable, and actively engaged with the audience. Companies where CEOs, founders, or executives interact with customers, whether through social media, direct responses to feedback, or participation in company events create an atmosphere of transparency and authenticity. When customers see that leadership is not distant or detached but instead personally invested in their experience, they develop a deeper emotional bond with the company.

Leaders also influence loyalty by shaping company policies that prioritize customer well-being over profit maximization. Many businesses lose customers not because their products are bad, but because they implement policies that make customer interactions frustrating or exploitative. Hidden fees, complicated return processes, poor warranty support, and aggressive upselling all signal to customers that the company does not truly value them. Leaders who take a long-term view and design policies that make it easy for customers to engage, purchase, return, and resolve issues create a foundation of goodwill that fosters enduring loyalty.

A customer-centric leader understands that loyalty is not just about keeping people from leaving, it is about making them feel emotionally invested in the brand. When customers feel valued, respected, and genuinely appreciated, they do not just continue buying from a company; they become advocates who spread positive word-of-mouth and defend the brand in public spaces. Leadership that focuses on deepening this connection through community engagement, rewards programs, and ongoing interaction ensures that customers become lifelong supporters.

Strong leadership also fosters a culture of continuous learning and improvement. Companies that remain customer favorites for years are those that never stop listening, never stop improving, and never take loyalty for granted. Leaders who actively seek customer feedback, analyze behavior patterns, and adjust their strategies accordingly create businesses that grow alongside their audience. They understand that what customers value today may not be what they value five years from now, and they ensure that their brands remain adaptable and responsive.

The most lasting customer loyalty is not transactional, it is emotional. People do not stay loyal to brands because they offer occasional discounts or rewards; they stay because they feel a genuine connection to the business. That connection is built and sustained by leadership that makes customer well-being a core business philosophy rather than a secondary priority.

Leadership-driven loyalty is what separates companies that survive from those that thrive. In industries where competition is fierce, businesses with loyal customers have a competitive advantage that cannot be easily copied. Competitors can imitate products, undercut prices, and copy marketing strategies, but they cannot replicate the deep emotional loyalty that a brand earns through strong leadership.

6.1 Leading by Example

Leadership is the invisible force that shapes customer loyalty in ways that go beyond policies and strategies. A leader's values, decision-making style, and overall business philosophy influence how employees engage with customers, how products evolve, and how a brand earns its place in the hearts of consumers. While many businesses focus on marketing to retain customers, the most enduring loyalty is cultivated through leadership that prioritizes customer well-being, trust, and consistent value delivery.

One of the key aspects of leadership that impacts customer loyalty is **leading by example**. Employees take their cues from management, and when leaders demonstrate a genuine commitment to customer satisfaction, that commitment filters down into every level of the organization. A leader who actively engages with customers takes the time to understand their needs and fosters a company culture that prioritizes service excellence and sets a precedent for employees to follow. In contrast, leadership that is disconnected from customer concerns, focused solely on financial metrics, or indifferent to service quality breeds an organization where customer loyalty is an afterthought rather than a priority.

Another major factor is decision-making transparency. Customers today value honesty and accountability from the businesses they support. Leaders who make an effort to communicate openly about company policies, product changes, and service improvements build trust with their audience. When customers understand the reasoning behind certain business decisions, whether it's a price adjustment, a product recall, or a new policy, they are more likely to remain loyal. However, when leadership makes abrupt changes without explanation, customers feel blindsided and lose confidence in the brand.

The ability to build emotional connections with customers is another hallmark of leadership that fosters loyalty. People do not remain loyal to businesses simply because of convenience or price; they stay because they feel a genuine connection with the brand. This connection is built when leadership ensures that customers feel heard, valued, and respected. A leader who takes the time to engage with customers through direct communication, social media interactions, or personal responses to feedback fosters a sense of community that strengthens brand attachment.

6.2 Crisis Management

Another essential quality of strong leadership is resilience in crisis management. Every company faces challenges, but how leadership responds determines whether customer trust is strengthened or eroded. Businesses that acknowledge mistakes, take responsibility, and actively work to resolve issues often earn even greater loyalty from customers. On the other hand, companies that avoid accountability, ignore customer concerns, or attempt to shift blame risk long-term reputational damage. Customers respect businesses that handle adversity with honesty and integrity, and they reward those that demonstrate a commitment to making things right.

Effective leaders also understand the importance of sustained engagement with their audience. Loyalty is not built through a single positive experience; it requires continuous effort. Businesses that check in with customers, send personalized messages, and make an effort to keep the relationship active beyond transactions see far greater retention rates. This engagement can come in many forms, such as exclusive offers for returning customers, personalized recommendations based on past interactions, or simply acknowledging loyal customers through appreciation programs. Leadership that prioritizes long-term engagement over short-term sales numbers builds brands that customers stick with for years.

Another crucial element of leadership in customer loyalty is **innovation with purpose**. Companies that remain stagnant eventually lose relevance, no matter how strong their brand once was. However, businesses that innovate thoughtfully ensuring that new products, services, and experiences align with customer needs maintain their competitive edge. Leaders who prioritize customer-driven innovation constantly seek ways to improve offerings based on real feedback rather than chasing industry trends for the sake of appearing modern. A company that listens to customers, implements improvements, and stays ahead of their evolving expectations demonstrates a commitment to long-term value creation.

A critical but often overlooked aspect of leadership's role in customer loyalty is ethical decision making. Customers today care about how businesses operate behind the scenes. Leadership that ensures fair wages for employees, engages in sustainable practices, and maintains ethical supply chains earns a different kind of loyalty, one that is based not just on quality but on shared values. Customers want to support companies that align with their personal beliefs, and businesses that embrace ethical leadership strengthen their emotional bond with their audience.

Trust is the foundation of customer loyalty, and leadership plays the most significant role in building and maintaining that trust. Every decision, communication, and action taken by a company's leadership contributes to how customers perceive their reliability and integrity. When leaders prioritize transparency, consistency, and customer satisfaction above immediate profits, they create brands that people feel proud to support. Customers who trust a business do not just continue buying from it, they actively defend it, recommend it, and become part of its community.

CHAPTER SEVEN

TURNING LOYAL CUSTOMERS INTO BRAND ADVOCATES

Loyal customers are the foundation of a successful business, but their true value goes beyond repeat purchases. The most powerful asset any company can have been a customer base that actively promotes its products and services. Businesses that understand the power of advocacy do not just focus on retaining customers, they turn them into vocal supporters who willingly spread the brand's message. This transformation from loyal customer to brand advocate does not happen by chance; it is the result of deliberate strategies that deepen emotional connections, encourage engagement, and create experiences worth sharing.

Customers become advocates when they feel a strong emotional connection to a brand. This connection is built over time through consistently positive experiences, genuine appreciation, and a shared sense of identity with the brand. People do not recommend products or services simply because they are satisfied; they do so because they believe in the brand and want others to experience the same benefits. Companies that prioritize emotional engagement create a community of advocates who promote the brand out of genuine enthusiasm rather than obligation.

One of the key drivers of advocacy is customer empowerment. Customers are more likely to talk about a brand when they feel like they are an integral part of its story. Businesses that involve customers in decision-making, seek their feedback, and recognize their contributions create a sense of belonging that fosters advocacy. This can be done through customer advisory boards, beta testing programs, and exclusive insider communities where loyal customers get early access to new products or services. When customers feel that their opinions shape the brand's future, they become personally invested in its success.

Another way to encourage advocacy is by making it easy for customers to share their experiences. Businesses that provide tools for customers to refer friends, leave reviews, and share their stories on social media create natural pathways for advocacy. Referral programs that reward customers for introducing new buyers, user-generated content campaigns, and branded hashtags that encourage customers to showcase their experiences are all effective ways to amplify customer voices. Companies that streamline the sharing process, whether through automated referral links, engaging social content, or interactive contests, see significantly higher levels of organic brand promotion.

Trust is at the core of advocacy. People only recommend brands they truly believe in because their own reputation is on the line when they do. Companies that want to convert loyal customers into advocates must ensure that their products, services, and customer experiences consistently exceed expectations. A customer who has had an exceptional experience with a brand is naturally inclined to talk about it, just as a customer who has had a terrible experience will eagerly share their dissatisfaction. Every interaction with a customer is an opportunity to reinforce trust and increase the likelihood of advocacy.

Customer recognition plays a significant role in advocacy as well. People love to be acknowledged, and businesses that take the time to appreciate their loyal customers often see higher levels of engagement. Simple gestures like personalized thank-you messages, loyalty rewards, and exclusive perks make customers feel valued and deepen their connection to the brand. Some of the most successful advocacy-driven businesses create VIP programs where top customers receive unique benefits, such as exclusive access to events, priority support, or limited-edition products. When customers feel like they are part of something special, they are far more likely to recommend the brand to others.

Businesses that actively encourage storytelling see some of the highest levels of customer advocacy. People connect through stories, and when brands provide platforms for customers to share their experiences, they create authentic, trust-building narratives that resonate with potential buyers. Companies that feature customer testimonials, case studies, or even customer-created blog posts and videos benefit from the credibility of real-world experiences. Advocacy thrives when customers feel proud to share how a brand has positively impacted their lives.

A powerful driver of advocacy is creating unforgettable moments. People remember and talk about experiences that stand out. Whether it is a handwritten note in a package, an unexpected upgrade, or a personalized follow-up after a purchase, these small moments of delight leave a lasting impression. Customers who experience thoughtful, unexpected gestures from a brand are more likely to tell others about it, not because they were asked to, but because the experience was genuinely worth sharing.

Social proof is a crucial element in customer advocacy. People are more likely to trust recommendations from their peers than from traditional advertising. Companies that showcase customer reviews, user-generated content, and influencer endorsements build credibility and encourage further advocacy. Businesses that actively engage with customer reviews—responding to positive feedback with appreciation and addressing concerns transparently—create a brand image that is trustworthy and responsive. When potential customers see real people advocating for a brand, they are far more likely to convert.

A structured referral program is one of the most effective ways to turn customers into advocates. Word-of-mouth recommendations are powerful, and businesses that incentivize referrals see increased engagement. A well-designed referral program should feel natural and rewarding rather than forced. Offering discounts, free products, or even charitable donations in exchange for referrals can motivate customers to actively introduce others to the brand. However, the best referral programs succeed because customers already believe in the brand—not just because they want a reward. The key is to create a referral system that aligns with the brand's values and feels genuine rather than transactional.

Community-building is another essential component of customer advocacy. When customers feel like they are part of a larger movement or shared identity, they develop a deeper emotional investment in the brand. Companies that create brand communities, whether through exclusive forums, online groups, or local events, see significantly higher levels of customer retention and advocacy. These communities give customers a space to connect, share experiences, and reinforce their loyalty to the brand. A strong brand community transforms customers from individual buyers into a collective force that actively promotes and defends the business.

One of the most underrated yet powerful ways to drive advocacy is co-creation. Brands that invite customers to contribute ideas, design new products, or participate in marketing campaigns create a sense of ownership among their audience. Customers who feel personally involved in a brand's success are more likely to advocate for it because they see themselves as stakeholders rather than just buyers. Businesses that have successfully implemented co-creation strategies, whether through crowdsourced product designs, fan-driven marketing campaigns, or collaborative innovations build a customer base that is emotionally invested in spreading the brand's message.

Turning loyal customers into brand advocates requires more than just good service; it requires a deliberate effort to deepen relationships, empower customers, and create experiences worth talking about. Advocacy is driven by emotional connection, trust, and a sense of belonging. Companies that master the art of customer advocacy do not just retain customers; they create a passionate community of supporters who actively spread the brand's message.

The transformation of loyal customers into brand advocates is one of the most powerful yet often overlooked aspects of business success. A loyal customer keeps returning to a brand, but an advocate actively promotes it, influencing others through word-of-mouth, social proof, and personal endorsements. While many companies invest heavily in marketing to attract new customers, the most successful businesses recognize that their greatest promotional asset is their existing customer base. Advocacy is not something that happens by accident, it is the result of thoughtful engagement, emotional investment, and creating experiences worth sharing.

A major reason customers become advocates is their emotional connection to a brand. People do not advocate for brands simply because they offer good products; they advocate for brands that align with their values, make them feel appreciated, and create positive experiences. This is why some of the most vocal brand advocates are not just repeat buyers but passionate believers in the brand's mission and identity. Companies that want to cultivate advocacy must go beyond transactions and focus on fostering deep emotional engagement with their audience.

One of the best ways to encourage advocacy is to involve customers in the brand's journey. People love to feel like they are part of something bigger than themselves, and brands that offer customers a role in shaping their identity create stronger bonds. Businesses that engage their most loyal customers in product development, seek their input on upcoming launches, or invite them to exclusive events make them feel like insiders rather than just buyers. This sense of participation turns customers into invested stakeholders in the brand's success, making them more likely to share and recommend it.

Encouraging organic storytelling is another powerful strategy. Customers relate best to real-life experiences, and when they see others sharing authentic testimonials, they feel more inclined to do the same. Instead of forcing testimonials, businesses should create environments where customers naturally want to talk about their experiences. Whether it is through social media challenges, user-generated content campaigns, or featured customer success stories, brands that actively highlight real customer voices amplify advocacy in a way that feels genuine and compelling.

People are also more likely to advocate for a brand when they receive unexpected value. Customers expect a product or service to meet their needs, but when a company exceeds those expectations, whether through an unexpected gift, a handwritten thank-you note, or proactive customer service, they feel compelled to share their positive experience. Small, thoughtful gestures can have a massive impact on word-of-mouth marketing. Customers who experience moments of surprise and delight are far more likely to tell friends, leave positive reviews, and promote the brand on social media.

Businesses must also make it effortless for customers to share their experiences. Many satisfied customers are willing to recommend a brand but do not always take the initiative to do so. Brands that streamline the process by offering simple referral programs, easy-to-use social sharing tools, and incentives for user-generated content significantly increase advocacy. A well-structured referral system does not just reward the referrer; it also provides an incentive for new customers to try the brand, creating a continuous cycle of advocacy-driven growth.

Community-building is another critical driver of advocacy. People naturally gravitate toward shared experiences, and brands that foster a sense of community among their customers see far higher levels of engagement. Whether through exclusive online groups, customer appreciation events, or branded forums, creating spaces where customers can interact deepens their emotional investment in the brand. A strong brand community transforms casual buyers into passionate brand supporters who feel connected not only to the business but also to other like-minded customers.

Advocacy also thrives on recognition and appreciation. Customers who feel valued are far more likely to go out of their way to promote a brand. Companies that publicly acknowledge their top customers, whether through special features, VIP programs, or personalized messages reinforce loyalty and encourage further engagement. This kind of personal recognition turns advocacy into a status symbol, where customers take pride in their relationship with the brand and actively seek opportunities to showcase their support.

Another overlooked yet highly effective way to encourage advocacy is through co-creation. Brands that invite customers to contribute to product designs, marketing campaigns, or creative ideas create a sense of ownership among their audience. When customers see their input reflected in a brand's final product or messaging, they feel a personal connection that naturally leads to advocacy. Whether it is through crowdsourced ideas, fan-driven branding initiatives, or interactive engagement campaigns, co-creation strengthens the emotional bond between customers and the business.

In today's digital world, social proof and credibility are more important than ever. Customers trust recommendations from their peers more than any advertisement, and businesses that actively highlight positive customer experiences leverage the power of trust-based marketing. Encouraging and featuring customer reviews, testimonials, and influencer collaborations amplifies advocacy in a way that is both persuasive and authentic. Customers who see real people benefiting from a brand are far more likely to advocate for it themselves.

While incentives like discounts, loyalty points, or exclusive offers can encourage advocacy, they should never be the sole motivator. Advocacy must be built on genuine enthusiasm, not just financial incentives. Brands that create advocacy through emotional engagement, shared identity, and exceptional experiences see far more sustainable word-of-mouth growth than those that rely solely on reward-based referrals. The goal should be to make customers want to share, not feel obligated to do so.

Consistency is another key factor in advocacy. Customers will only continue recommending a brand if they believe in its reliability and credibility. A company that is inconsistent in service, product quality, or customer engagement will struggle to maintain advocacy. Customers do not just advocate for a brand because of a single positive experience, they do so because they trust that the brand will deliver excellence every time. Companies that ensure consistent, high-quality experiences reinforce customer confidence and make advocacy a natural extension of loyalty.

Customer advocacy is the pinnacle of brand loyalty. It is the stage where customers go from being passive buyers to active promoters who voluntarily spread the brand's message. This transition is not accidental—it results from consistent positive experiences, emotional attachment, and a brand that aligns with the customer's identity and values. Businesses that successfully turn customers into advocates enjoy a unique advantage: they generate organic, word-of-mouth marketing that is more powerful than any paid advertisement.

One of the most important yet often overlooked aspects of advocacy is emotional resonance. Customers advocate for brands that make them feel something personal, special, or transformative. People are far more likely to recommend a brand if it has helped them overcome a problem, given them a unique experience, or contributed positively to their identity. For example, a fitness brand that helps customers achieve their health goals does more than sell workout gear—it becomes part of their success story. Similarly, a skincare brand that restores confidence in its users fosters a deeper emotional connection that goes beyond the product itself. When customers see a brand as part of their journey, they naturally share their experience with others.

Advocacy is strongest when customers see a brand as an extension of themselves. People love to associate with brands that reflect their personality, beliefs, and aspirations. This is why certain brands develop cult-like followings, where customers do not just buy the products— they adopt the brand as part of their lifestyle.

Companies that understand identity-based advocacy create exclusive brand cultures that customers feel proud to be part of. Apple, for instance, has built a community where users feel a strong sense of belonging, to the extent that iPhone owners often advocate for Apple products without being asked. Similarly, luxury brands like Rolex and Louis Vuitton cultivate an aspirational image that makes customers eager to promote their association with the brand.

For businesses looking to leverage identity-based advocacy, it is important to give customers reasons to associate themselves with the brand on a deeper level. This can be done through storytelling, brand mission, and shared values. A brand that stands for sustainability, for instance, will naturally attract eco-conscious advocates who proudly share their purchases as a reflection of their commitment to the environment. A company that champions diversity and inclusion will find its most loyal customers becoming advocates because they align with the brand's core beliefs.

Beyond values, companies can reinforce advocacy through exclusive communities. When customers feel like insiders, they develop a stronger sense of commitment to the brand. Creating VIP customer groups, loyalty clubs, or ambassador programs fosters a feeling of exclusivity and makes customers more eager to promote the brand. Exclusive access to events, early product releases, or private customer forums all contribute to making advocacy feel like a privilege rather than an obligation.

Another effective strategy in identity-based advocacy is leveraging social status. Customers love to share experiences that elevate their personal brand. Businesses that create limited-edition products, exclusive membership tiers, or influencer collaborations tap into the human desire for status recognition. When customers feel like their association with a brand increases their social credibility, they are more likely to advocate for it publicly.

7.1 The Psychological Triggers Behind Advocacy

Understanding the psychology behind customer advocacy helps businesses proactively encourage organic promotion. There are several key psychological principles that drive advocacy:

The reciprocity principle plays a crucial role in advocacy. People feel naturally inclined to return a favor when they have received something valuable. When businesses go out of their way to provide exceptional service, thoughtful gestures, or unexpected perks, customers feel a subconscious obligation to give back—often in the form of referrals, testimonials, or positive reviews. This is why companies that prioritize customer appreciation through personalized thank-you messages, surprise gifts, or complimentary upgrades often see an increase in advocacy. Customers who feel valued want to reciprocate by sharing their positive experience.

The fear of missing out (FOMO) is another powerful trigger. Customers are more likely to advocate for a brand when they feel like they are part of an exclusive experience that others are missing out on. Limited-time offers, invitation-only memberships, and product drops create urgency and social appeal. Businesses that use scarcity marketing—whether through limited-edition products, waitlist access, or VIP-only content—tap into customers' natural desire to be part of something special. When customers experience something unique and rare, they become eager to share it with their network.

The social validation effect also plays a significant role in advocacy. People are more likely to talk about a brand when they see others doing the same. This is why brands that create viral social media moments, influencer collaborations, or highly engaging customer challenges benefit from widespread advocacy. When a brand becomes a trend, customers do not want to be left out, leading to more organic recommendations and social shares.

Another psychological driver of advocacy is loss aversion. Customers who have developed a strong connection with a brand often feel the need to protect it. This is why brand advocates are willing to defend their favorite companies against criticism or negative feedback. Businesses that maintain consistent customer engagement, transparent communication, and a strong brand identity create advocates who actively protect and promote the brand's reputation.

7.2 The Future of Customer Advocacy and How Brands Can Stay Ahead

Customer advocacy is evolving with new digital trends, technology, and shifting consumer expectations. Businesses that wish to remain leaders in advocacy-driven growth must adapt to the changing landscape while staying true to their core values.

The rise of personalized digital experiences means that customers expect brands to know them on a deeper level. Businesses that use AI-driven recommendations, hyper-personalized loyalty programs, and customized communication create stronger relationships with customers. A brand that remembers a customer's past purchases, preferences, and behavior increases the likelihood of advocacy because it makes interactions feel tailored and thoughtful.

The power of micro-influencers is also reshaping advocacy. While celebrity endorsements remain influential, many brands are now recognizing the power of smaller, niche influencers who have highly engaged communities. Companies that partner with everyday customers who have authentic influence within their circles whether through referral networks, ambassador programs, or community leadership see higher engagement and more genuine advocacy.

Social commerce is also playing an increasing role in advocacy. Customers now share their brand experiences directly within shopping platforms, livestreams, and community-driven marketplaces. Businesses that integrate seamless sharing features within their shopping experiences such as one-click referral links, social media integration, and real-time testimonials make advocacy an effortless and natural part of the buying process.

The future of customer advocacy will be built on trust, personalization, and brand communities. Businesses that recognize the shift from transactional marketing to experience-driven, community-based engagement will thrive in the long term. Customers will continue advocating for brands that make them feel valued, connected, and part of something bigger than themselves.

Turning loyal customers into brand advocates is not a one-time effort, it is an ongoing relationship. Businesses that continue to nurture their advocates, recognize their contributions, and evolve with their needs will build a self-sustaining ecosystem of organic growth and influence. Advocacy is not just about spreading the word; it is about creating movements that customers feel deeply invested in. Brands that master this art will not only retain customers but also turn them into lifelong champions who fuel the company's success for years to come.

CHAPTER EIGHT

SUSTAINING LONG-TERM CUSTOMER RELATIONSHIPS

Building customer loyalty is not just about acquiring repeat business; it is about nurturing relationships that endure for years, even decades. Many businesses focus heavily on attracting new customers, but the real measure of success lies in how well a company retains and deepens its connection with existing customers. Long-term relationships are the foundation of sustainable growth, creating a customer base that is not only loyal but also engaged, enthusiastic, and willing to advocate for the brand.

Customer relationships, like any meaningful connection, require constant care, effort, and evolution. A brand that was once exciting can become stagnant if it does not continuously offer value, relevance, and emotional engagement. Businesses that sustain long-term customer relationships are those that recognize customer needs change over time and adapt their strategies accordingly. What kept a customer loyal five years ago may not be enough to keep them engaged today. This is why companies that stay ahead of customer expectations consistently maintain stronger, longer-lasting relationships.

One of the key elements in sustaining long-term relationships is understanding the full customer lifecycle. Businesses that only focus on the immediate transaction miss opportunities to build ongoing engagement that extends beyond a single purchase. Customers go through different phases from discovering a brand to making a purchase, becoming a loyal buyer, and eventually becoming an advocate. Each phase requires different levels of attention, communication, and value delivery. Companies that recognize these shifts and tailor their interactions accordingly create a seamless, evolving customer journey that strengthens relationships over time.

Consistency is critical in maintaining long-term customer relationships. Customers stay with brands that they trust to deliver the same level of quality, service, and engagement at every interaction. Businesses that frequently change pricing structures, product offerings, or customer service policies without considering the impact on their existing customers risk losing loyalty. Customers want reliability, they want to know that they can count on a brand to deliver what it promises, time and time again.

Another important factor is proactive engagement. Many businesses make the mistake of only reaching out to customers when they need something, whether it is a renewal, an upsell, or a re-engagement campaign. Customers can sense when a brand's interaction is purely transactional, and this can lead to disengagement. Companies that build long-term relationships find ways to connect with customers consistently, even when there is no immediate sale to be made. Personalized check-ins, educational content, exclusive updates, and thoughtful gestures show customers that the brand values them beyond their purchasing power.

Personalization plays a significant role in keeping customer relationships fresh and meaningful. Customers want to feel recognized, understood, and catered to. Generic mass emails or one-size-fits-all promotions do not create strong bonds. Businesses that use customer data to personalize interactions, whether through tailored recommendations, individualized offers, or customized experiences create stronger emotional connections. The more a brand can make a customer feel like their experience is uniquely crafted for them, the longer that relationship will last.

Trust remains the backbone of long-term customer relationships. Customers stay with brands that they believe in and feel secure with. This is why businesses that prioritize honesty, transparency, and ethical practices maintain stronger connections. Customers are not just buying products; they are investing in a brand's values, reliability, and the assurance that they will always be treated with respect. Brands that openly communicate changes, acknowledge mistakes, and consistently act with integrity solidify customer trust that lasts for years.

Beyond trust, long-term loyalty is sustained through customer empowerment. Businesses that give customers more control over their experiences build relationships that feel collaborative rather than one-sided. Whether it is through flexible subscription models, self-service options, personalized dashboards, or user-generated content initiatives, brands that empower customers to engage on their own terms create deeper, more meaningful connections.

Loyalty programs also play a major role in maintaining long-term relationships. However, not all loyalty programs are effective. Many businesses design programs that only reward transactions rather than engagement, advocacy, or long-term commitment. The best loyalty programs go beyond simple point systems and offer customers real, meaningful benefits, whether it is VIP treatment, early access to new products, personalized perks, or experiential rewards. Businesses that continuously evolve their loyalty programs based on customer preferences keep relationships dynamic and engaging.

Another key to sustaining long-term customer relationships is continual innovation. Customers are drawn to brands that stay relevant, introduce fresh ideas, and adapt to changing market conditions. Even if a business has a strong base of loyal customers, failing to innovate can lead to stagnation. Companies that consistently introduce new products, improve services, and enhance customer experiences keep long-term customers engaged and excited. The key is to evolve without losing the core identity and values that made customers loyal in the first place.

Community-building also plays a crucial role in keeping long-term relationships strong. Customers who feel connected to a larger community of like-minded individuals are more likely to stay loyal. Brands that foster customer communities, whether through online forums, social media engagement, or exclusive networking opportunities create a sense of belonging that makes customers feel like they are part of something bigger than just a buyer-seller relationship. Businesses that integrate community-driven initiatives, peer-to-peer interactions, and customer-led conversations develop relationships that are not just transactional but culturally and emotionally enriching.

One of the most overlooked yet effective ways to sustain customer relationships is through gratitude and appreciation. Customers want to feel valued, not just as buyers but as individuals who contribute to a brand's success. Brands that go out of their way to show appreciation whether through personalized thank-you notes, unexpected discounts, anniversary rewards, or public recognition strengthen their bonds with long-term customers. The more a brand shows genuine gratitude for customer loyalty, the more likely customers are to remain engaged.

At the heart of long-term customer relationships is the ability to adapt and listen. Customer needs change, industries evolve, and new challenges emerge. Businesses that remain rigid and unresponsive risk losing relevance. Brands that thrive in maintaining long-term relationships are those that actively listen to their customers, embrace feedback, and make improvements based on real customer insights. Customers appreciate brands that evolve with them, ensuring that their experiences remain aligned with their current expectations and lifestyle needs.

Long-term customer relationships are not built overnight. They require continuous engagement, value reinforcement, and a deep understanding of customer needs as they evolve over time. Businesses that sustain long-term relationships recognize that loyalty is not just about repeat purchases, it is about fostering a connection where customers feel understood, valued, and engaged at every stage of their journey.

Maintaining long-term customer relationships requires businesses to continuously innovate and deepen engagement. Customers today expect more than just good service; they want ongoing value, personalized experiences, and a brand that grows with them over time. Companies that fail to evolve their customer relationships risk losing even their most loyal patrons to competitors who offer fresh, relevant, and emotionally engaging experiences.

One of the most critical aspects of long-term customer retention is reinventing engagement strategies without losing core brand identity. Customers may stay with a brand because of familiarity, but they continue advocating for it when they see it as a dynamic force that adapts to their evolving needs, preferences, and aspirations. Businesses that successfully balance consistency with innovation create customer relationships that feel both reliable and exciting.

Transactional relationships are short-lived, but brands that cultivate emotional resonance create deep, lasting bonds with their customers. When customers feel emotionally connected to a brand, they are more likely to forgive minor mistakes, remain loyal despite competitive pricing, and actively engage with the brand beyond purchases. Emotional loyalty is far more enduring than habit-based or reward-driven loyalty because it is rooted in shared values, personal identity, and brand trust.

One-way businesses can strengthen emotional connections through storytelling. Customers do not just buy products; they invest in stories that align with their beliefs and aspirations. Brands that craft compelling narratives, whether through their origins, sustainability efforts, community involvement, or innovation create a sense of belonging that keeps customers engaged for years. A fitness brand, for example, can sustain long-term relationships by not just selling workout gear but by sharing real customer transformation stories, fitness journeys, and expert insights that resonate with the audience's goals.

Another way to deepen emotional engagement is by making brand interactions feel personal and human. Customers today are bombarded with automated responses and robotic interactions. Businesses that introduce human elements into digital experiences—such as personalized check-ins, handwritten notes, or direct interactions with brand leaders—stand out as brands that genuinely care. Small gestures, like a CEO personally responding to a long-time customer's tweet or a brand remembering a customer's anniversary with a special offer, create emotional moments that customers cherish and talk about.

8.1 Anticipating Customer Needs Before They Arise

Long-term customer relationships thrive when businesses can predict and address customer needs before they become concerns. Anticipation is a sign of deep understanding and proactive customer care, and brands that master this art create a seamless, stress-free experience that strengthens trust and loyalty.

One way to anticipate customer needs is by leveraging customer history and behavioral patterns. A business that tracks past interactions can predict when a customer might need a product refill, when they may be interested in an upgrade, or when they might be at risk of disengagement. Subscription-based services, for example, can offer preemptive renewals, personalized content recommendations, or timely upgrades that keep customers engaged without them having to take the first step.

Another way to anticipate customer needs is through proactive problem-solving. Instead of waiting for complaints, businesses should be actively identifying friction points and resolving them before they affect the customer experience. For example, if a brand notices a pattern of delayed shipments during certain months, it can notify customers ahead of time and offer solutions like faster delivery options. If customers frequently ask similar questions, brands can introduce intelligent, self-service resources that address concerns before they arise.

Anticipation also involves staying ahead of industry shifts and evolving consumer expectations. Customers' lifestyles change, and brands that are forward-thinking position themselves as trusted advisors rather than mere service providers. A tech company, for instance, can educate customers on upcoming industry changes that may impact their devices. A skincare brand can keep customers informed about new ingredients and trends tailored to their specific skin types. Businesses that act as customer educators and guides create relationships that go beyond transactions, they become indispensable partners in the customer's journey.

8.2 Sustaining Loyalty Through Continuous Reinvention

Loyalty should never feel static. A brand that delivers the same experience year after year without any evolution risks losing relevance. While consistency is important, long-term customer relationships flourish when a brand continuously improves, surprises, and delights.

One effective way to sustain long-term engagement is through periodic reinvention of loyalty programs. Many businesses launch loyalty programs only to let them stagnate, offering the same rewards and experiences for years. Customers, however, crave new challenges, exclusive experiences, and evolving benefits. The most successful loyalty programs introduce tiered structures, gamification, or seasonal rewards that keep engagement fresh. For example, a brand can introduce a surprise challenge every six months, where customers unlock a unique reward for engaging with the brand in a new way.

Another method of reinvention is refreshing brand messaging and gaining experiences while maintaining core values. Customers appreciate brands that stay modern, relevant, and forward-thinking. This can mean rebranding campaigns, interactive digital experiences, exclusive product drops, or behind-the-scenes insights into company innovations. A restaurant chain, for example, can retain long-term customers by introducing new menu items based on seasonal trends, keeping the experience exciting yet familiar.

Companies that expand their value proposition also sustain loyalty more effectively. Customers who initially purchased a product for one reason may develop new needs over time. A brand that introduces complementary services, additional benefits, or extended support systems keeps customers engaged for longer. For example, an online bookstore that initially sells books can expand its long-term value by offering personalized reading recommendations, virtual book clubs, or audiobook memberships.

One of the most powerful yet underutilized strategies for sustaining long-term relationships is creating rituals around the brand experience. Rituals are repeatable experiences that customers associate with a brand, reinforcing their sense of belonging and identity. Starbucks, for example, has ingrained the habit of personalized morning coffee routines into customers' lives, while brands like Nike integrate fitness into customers' daily routines through digital challenges and training programs. When a brand becomes woven into customers' everyday habits, loyalty transforms into lifestyle integration.

Sustaining long-term customer relationships requires more than just delivering great products and services, it demands continuous engagement, adaptation, and emotional connection. Businesses that remain proactive, forward-thinking, and customer-centric in their evolution create relationships that not only last but also deepen over time.

CHAPTER NINE

LEVERAGING DATA TO ENHANCE CUSTOMER LOYALTY

In today's digital-driven world, customer loyalty is no longer just about great service and consistent engagement is also about understanding customers at a deeper level through data. Businesses that leverage data-driven insights can create hyper-personalized experiences, anticipate customer needs, and refine loyalty strategies with precision. The ability to collect, analyze, and act on customer data has become a game-changer for sustaining long-term relationships and ensuring that customers remain engaged, satisfied, and emotionally connected to a brand.

Data-driven customer loyalty goes beyond tracking purchase history. It involves analyzing behavioral patterns, feedback loops, engagement trends, and predictive insights to create tailored experiences that feel uniquely crafted for each customer. When done effectively, data-driven loyalty strategies help businesses increase retention, improve customer satisfaction, and turn casual buyers into lifelong advocates.

One of the biggest challenges businesses face today is customer churn—losing customers who disengage over time. Many companies fail to recognize the warning signs of disengagement until it is too late. However, with the right data analytics tools, businesses can detect early signals of customer dissatisfaction and take proactive measures to retain them. Identifying patterns such as declining engagement, reduced purchase frequency, or negative sentiment in customer interactions allows businesses to step in with personalized offers, loyalty incentives, or direct communication to re-engage customers before they leave.

One of the most powerful uses of data in customer loyalty is hyper-personalization. Today's consumers expect brands to understand their preferences, anticipate their needs, and deliver experiences tailored to their unique behaviors. Businesses that still rely on generic promotions, mass email campaigns, and broad marketing strategies risk alienating customers who now demand individualized attention.

Using customer data, businesses can segment their audience based on behavior, preferences, demographics, and engagement levels. This allows for more precise targeting and messaging. For instance, a retail brand that tracks browsing history and past purchases can send personalized recommendations that align with a customer's style preferences. A streaming service can curate movie or music playlists based on a user's watching or listening habits, making the experience feel deeply relevant and intuitive.

Beyond product recommendations, data-driven personalization can enhance customer interactions at every touchpoint. Chatbots powered by AI can offer real-time support based on previous inquiries, ensuring that customers receive fast, relevant assistance. Automated email sequences can adjust based on customer behavior, sending different messages depending on whether a customer is actively engaged or has been inactive for a certain period. Personalization should not feel like a marketing gimmick—it should feel seamless and natural, giving customers the sense that the brand truly understands them.

One of the most transformative aspects of data-driven loyalty is predictive analytics, which enables businesses to forecast customer behaviors and proactively enhance their experience. By analyzing past interactions, purchase trends, and engagement patterns, businesses can predict when a customer might need a service renewal, when they are likely to upgrade a product, or when they are at risk of disengagement.

For example, an airline that uses predictive analytics can determine when a frequent traveler is due for another trip based on past booking behavior. By sending timely, personalized offers, the airline increases the likelihood of repeat business. Similarly, an e-commerce company can analyze cart abandonment data and trigger automated reminders or limited-time discounts to encourage customers to complete their purchases.

Predictive analytics also plays a crucial role in customer retention. Businesses can identify at-risk customers who show signs of declining engagement—and intervene before they churn. If a loyal customer who once purchased monthly has not made a purchase in six months, an automated system can send a customized incentive to re-engage them, such as a loyalty discount or a message highlighting new arrivals that match their interests.

By leveraging machine learning algorithms and AI-driven insights, companies can go beyond reactive customer service and shift toward proactive engagement, ensuring that customers remain engaged long before they even consider switching brands.

Loyalty is not static—it requires constant refinement and adaptation. Businesses that rely on real-time customer feedback loops have a greater ability to identify issues, improve service quality, and maintain customer satisfaction.

Customer surveys, Net Promoter Scores (NPS), online reviews, and social media interactions all provide valuable insights into how customers feel about a brand at any given moment. Businesses that actively listen to this feedback—and more importantly, act on it—show customers that their opinions matter.

One effective strategy is closed-loop feedback systems, where businesses not only collect customer feedback but also follow up with resolutions or improvements. If a customer leaves a negative review about a delayed delivery, a brand that reaches out to acknowledge the issue, provide a compensation offer, and implement better shipping policies creates a lasting impression that can turn dissatisfaction into renewed loyalty.

Real-time sentiment analysis, powered by AI, can also help brands monitor social media and customer interactions to gauge brand perception. If a company notices a spike in complaints about a specific issue, it can respond quickly, address concerns, and prevent further customer dissatisfaction before it escalates.

Loyalty programs have evolved from simple points-based systems to intelligent, data-driven engagement platforms. Traditional loyalty programs often fail because they treat all customers the same, offering generic rewards that may not be meaningful to every individual. However, by leveraging data insights, businesses can create dynamic, highly personalized loyalty programs that cater to each customer's unique behaviors and preferences.

A tiered loyalty system, for instance, can be structured based on customer activity levels. High-spending customers might unlock exclusive experiences, VIP customer service, or early access to new products, while casual buyers receive rewards tailored to their engagement patterns. Data-driven loyalty programs also allow businesses to adjust rewards in real-time based on customer activity. If a once-loyal customer begins spending less, the system can offer a targeted incentive to rekindle their engagement.

Businesses that integrate AI-powered loyalty platforms can also analyze purchasing cycles, preferred communication channels, and spending habits to craft offers that feel truly valuable. The more precisely tailored a loyalty program is, the more effective it becomes in driving long-term retention.

While data-driven customer loyalty offers immense potential, ethical data usage is critical. Customers are increasingly concerned about data privacy, security, and how their personal information is being used. Brands that fail to handle data responsibly risk losing customer trust, damaging their reputation, and facing regulatory challenges.

To build trust, businesses must be transparent about their data collection practices. Customers should always know what data is being collected, how it is being used, and what benefits they receive in return. Implementing opt-in policies, clear privacy settings, and easy data control options empowers customers and reinforces their confidence in the brand.

A company that demonstrates ethical data handling, prioritizes customer consent, and openly communicates its data security measures will not only retain customer trust but also strengthen long-term loyalty. Customers who feel safe and respected in their data interactions are far more likely to remain engaged, continue sharing insights, and deepen their relationship with the brand.

In the modern business landscape, data is not just a tool, it is the foundation of customer loyalty. Businesses that effectively harness customer insights, predictive analytics, and real-time feedback systems create experiences that feel personal, relevant, and proactive.

By using data to anticipate needs, personalize interactions, and refine loyalty strategies, companies turn customers into long-term partners who feel understood, valued, and consistently engaged. Brands that balance technological innovation with ethical, customer-first values will lead the future of loyalty-driven business growth.

The role of data in enhancing customer loyalty is undeniable in today's digital economy. Businesses that rely on guesswork to retain customers will always struggle against those that make data-driven decisions to personalize interactions, anticipate needs, and refine engagement strategies. Data allows companies to transition from a reactive approach to a proactive one, identifying early warning signs of disengagement and addressing them before customers leave. It enables businesses to create customized experiences that resonate with individuals rather than relying on generic, mass-marketed approaches. In a world where customers expect brands to know them, remember them, and cater to their preferences, data becomes the foundation for meaningful, long-term relationships.

One of the greatest advantages of using data in customer loyalty is the ability to track behavioral patterns and use them to predict future actions. Customers leave digital footprints in every interaction they have with a brand, from their browsing history and purchasing habits to their feedback on customer service interactions. When analyzed properly, this data provides insights into their needs, preferences, and potential pain points. Businesses that can recognize these patterns can tailor their engagement strategies accordingly, whether it's by sending personalized product recommendations, offering timely discounts before a customer considers switching to a competitor, or providing proactive support before an issue escalates into frustration. The ability to foresee customer needs and address them before the customer even voices them creates a sense of trust and reliability that strengthens loyalty over time.

Personalization is one of the most powerful applications of data in building customer loyalty. Gone are the days when simply addressing a customer by name in an email was enough to be considered personalization. Today's consumers expect interactions that feel uniquely tailored to them, based on their past experiences, behaviors, and preferences. A customer who frequently buys running shoes from a sports brand should not receive generic promotional emails about basketball gear, but rather recommendations for running accessories, exclusive deals on new models, or content related to improving running performance. When brands make customers feel like they are understood on a personal level, they create an emotional bond that goes beyond transactional loyalty. Personalized experiences show customers that they are not just another number in the system but value individuals whose preferences matter.

Predictive analytics takes personalization a step further by allowing businesses to anticipate what customers will need next based on historical data. Subscription-based services, for example, can analyze usage patterns and proactively remind customers to renew before their subscription expires, reducing churn. A grocery delivery service can suggest items that a customer frequently orders, making their shopping experience more convenient. A luxury brand can recognize a high-value customer's purchasing frequency and extend a personalized invitation to an exclusive event just before they reach the decision-making stage for their next big purchase. This type of engagement makes customers feel like their relationship with the brand is seamless and effortless, encouraging them to stay loyal.

Customer loyalty programs also benefit significantly from data-driven insights. Traditional loyalty programs often fail because they take a one-size-fits-all approach, offering generic points and rewards that may not appeal to every customer. However, data enables businesses to create loyalty programs that are dynamic, adaptive, and personalized to each individual's preferences. A restaurant chain can analyze a customer's ordering habits and offer a reward for their favorite meal rather than a random discount. A fashion retailer can track seasonal purchase trends and offer early access to new arrivals in a customer's preferred style. A travel company can recognize a frequent traveler's favorite destinations and offer personalized deals that align with their travel history. These tailored rewards make customers feel that their loyalty is genuinely appreciated and that they are receiving exclusive benefits that matter to them.

Another crucial aspect of leveraging data for customer loyalty is real-time feedback and sentiment analysis. Businesses that actively listen to their customers and respond accordingly build stronger relationships and increase satisfaction. Surveys, reviews, and social media interactions provide valuable insights into how customers feel about a brand at any given moment. If a business detects a surge in negative feedback about a particular product or service, it can take immediate action to rectify the issue before it leads to mass dissatisfaction. Brands that show they are responsive to customer concerns, rather than ignoring them, earn trust and credibility. Closing the feedback loop by acknowledging customer concerns, implementing improvements, and informing customers of the changes made as a result of their feedback demonstrates that the company genuinely values its relationship with them.

One of the most overlooked benefits of using data in customer loyalty is its ability to create frictionless experiences. Customers today value convenience, and any barriers to engagement can lead to frustration and eventual disengagement. Data helps businesses streamline interactions by reducing redundant steps, automating processes, and ensuring that customers receive the most relevant information when they need it. A seamless checkout experience, for example, can be created by remembering a customer's preferred payment method and shipping address. A support team that has access to a customer's history can provide faster, more accurate solutions without requiring the customer to repeat themselves. A mobile app that offers personalized in-app recommendations based on usage behavior creates a more intuitive experience that keeps customers engaged. When interactions are effortless and intuitive, customers are more likely to stay loyal because they associate the brand with ease and efficiency.

However, while data provides endless opportunities to enhance customer loyalty, it must be used ethically and responsibly. Customers today are more aware than ever of data privacy concerns, and businesses that mishandle data risk not only regulatory consequences but also damage their reputation and loss of customer trust. Transparency is key customers should always be informed about what data is being collected, how it is being used, and what benefits they receive in exchange. Brands that offer customers control over their data, such as allowing them to opt in or out of certain types of tracking or communications, create a relationship based on mutual respect. Customers are more willing to share data with brands that they trust, but that trust must be earned through honesty, security, and responsible data practices.

The integration of artificial intelligence and machine learning is further revolutionizing how data is used to enhance customer loyalty. AI-powered chatbots, predictive product recommendations, and automated customer service interactions are becoming increasingly sophisticated, offering real-time personalization on a scale. Machine learning algorithms can continuously analyze customer behaviors and refine engagement strategies without human intervention, ensuring that loyalty efforts are always optimized. While automation can enhance efficiency, it is important to maintain a balance between technology and human touch. Customers still appreciate authentic, human interactions, especially when dealing with complex issues or emotional concerns. The most successful brands combine the power of data and AI with personalized, human-led engagement to create loyalty strategies that feel both advanced and deeply personal.

The transformative power of data in enhancing customer loyalty cannot be overstated. In a world where consumers have endless choices, businesses that use data to create intelligent, seamless, and emotionally engaging customer experiences stand out. The ability to collect and analyze customer data in real time allows companies to anticipate needs, personalize interactions, and continuously refine engagement strategies. However, while data provides limitless possibilities, it must be used with precision, responsibility, and a deep understanding of human behavior. A data-driven approach to loyalty is not just about numbers; it is about using those numbers to create genuine connections, memorable interactions, and a customer journey that feels intuitive and rewarding.

9.1 The Role of Behavioral Insights in Customer Loyalty

Data-driven loyalty does not rely solely on purchase history. While knowing what customers buy is important, understanding why they buy is even more valuable. Businesses that take a deep dive into behavioral analytics can uncover patterns, motivations, and emotional triggers that drive customer decisions.

Behavioral insights allow businesses to recognize the key moments when customer engagement peaks and when it declines. A fashion retailer, for example, may notice that customers engage heavily with their online store during seasonal changes but drop off at other times. Using this data, the retailer can create seasonal engagement campaigns, personalized style recommendations, and exclusive promotions tailored to each customer's shopping cycle. Similarly, a streaming service can track which types of content a user enjoys most and use that information to provide tailored recommendations that keep the user coming back.

Another significant advantage of behavioral insights is the ability to create dynamic customer journeys. Instead of using a fixed loyalty funnel where every customer follows the same path, businesses can adapt their engagement strategies in real time based on each individual's preferences and actions. For instance, if a customer frequently engages with educational content but has not yet made a purchase, a brand can offer free trials, exclusive webinars, or personalized consultation sessions to guide them toward conversion. By adapting to behavioral signals, companies create experiences that feel effortless and naturally aligned with each customer's decision-making process.

Beyond engagement, behavioral analytics also helps brands detect signs of customer fatigue or potential churn. If a once-loyal customer starts spending less time interacting with a brand's app, emails, or website, the system can trigger personalized re-engagement efforts. A customer who has not opened a promotional email in months should not receive generic discounts but rather a message tailored to reignite their interest based on their last meaningful interaction with the brand. This proactive approach ensures that companies retain customers before disengagement turns into complete abandonment.

9.2 The Intersection of Emotional Intelligence and Data-Driven Loyalty

While data provides quantitative insights into customer behavior, emotional intelligence bridges the gap between numbers and human connection. Businesses that use data solely for automation and efficiency may find short-term gains, but lasting customer loyalty is built on empathy, emotional resonance, and meaningful engagement.

One of the most effective ways to integrate emotional intelligence into data-driven strategies is through sentiment analysis. Companies that monitor customer sentiment through social media, online reviews, and customer service interactions can gauge real-time emotions and adjust their approach accordingly. If a brand detects a surge in negative sentiment, it can respond immediately with genuine apologies, corrective actions, and enhanced customer support to rebuild trust. On the other hand, if a brand sees positive sentiment, it can capitalize on that momentum by rewarding loyal customers with exclusive perks, featuring user-generated content, or strengthening community engagement.

Emotionally intelligent businesses also recognize that not all customers respond to incentives in the same way. While some customers are motivated by discounts and rewards, others value experiences, recognition, or social impact. A brand that takes the time to understand what drives individual customers can tailor its loyalty strategies accordingly. A high-end luxury brand, for example, may find that exclusivity and status-based rewards drive loyalty more than percentage discounts. In contrast, a sustainability-focused brand may discover that charitable donations or eco-friendly initiatives are more effective in retaining its audience.

Another essential aspect of emotional intelligence in data-driven loyalty is the power of storytelling. Customers do not just want to buy from brands, they want to feel connected to their mission, values, and purpose. Data can help businesses identify which stories resonate most with their audience and tailor their messaging accordingly. If analytics reveal that customers engage most with content that highlights social impact, a brand can incorporate more behind-the-scenes narratives about its ethical sourcing, sustainability efforts, or community initiatives. This strengthens the emotional connection between the brand and its customers, making loyalty feel organic rather than incentivized.

Furthermore, businesses that understand the psychology of reciprocity can use data to enhance their customer appreciation strategies. When customers feel genuinely valued and appreciated, they are more likely to remain loyal. A personalized thank-you message, a surprise birthday gift, or an exclusive early access invitation can have a greater impact on long-term retention than any generic marketing campaign. Data allows companies to execute these gestures at scale, ensuring that appreciation feels authentic and meaningful rather than automated and transactional.

CHAPTER TEN

FUTURE-PROOFING CUSTOMER LOYALTY IN A CHANGING WORLD

Customer loyalty is not static, it evolves alongside shifts in technology, consumer behavior, economic trends, and cultural expectations. Businesses that rely on outdated loyalty strategies risk losing relevance as customers seek brands that align with their values, priorities, and lifestyles. The brands that thrive in the future will not just react to changes; they will anticipate them, adapting their loyalty programs, customer engagement strategies, and brand positioning to remain indispensable. Future-proofing customer loyalty requires a blend of agility, innovation, and a deep commitment to continuous value creation.

One of the most significant challenges businesses face today is the shortening attention span of consumers. With an overwhelming number of brands competing for engagement, customer relationships must be nurtured in ways that feel meaningful, effortless, and rewarding. Loyalty is no longer just about rewards programs—it is about creating emotional connections, seamless experiences, and personalized engagement that keeps customers coming back, even when competitors offer similar or cheaper alternatives. Brands that fail to differentiate themselves beyond price and convenience will struggle to maintain loyalty in the long run.

To future-proof customer relationships, businesses must first recognize that loyalty today is fluid rather than fixed. Customers no longer commit to brands for life simply out of habit or tradition. Instead, they remain loyal when they feel consistently valued, heard, and engaged. A company that builds strong emotional bonds with its audience is far more likely to retain customers, even when faced with market disruptions, economic downturns, or new competitors. This requires a long-term vision for customer engagement that goes beyond short-term promotions or transactional benefits.

Personalization will continue to be a driving force in customer loyalty, but the future of personalization will be about context-aware, real-time engagement rather than basic name-based customization. As artificial intelligence and machine learning become more sophisticated, brands will be able to anticipate customer needs with unprecedented accuracy. Businesses that implement AI-driven personalization will create experiences that feel intuitive, adjusting recommendations, communications, and rewards in real time based on each customer's behavior, mood, and preferences. A retail brand, for example, could use predictive analytics to send personalized style recommendations the moment a customer starts browsing, rather than waiting for them to make a purchase. A hospitality brand could anticipate a traveler's preferences based on past stays and automatically adjust their experience—from room preferences to dining recommendations—without them having to ask. The future of loyalty will be about anticipation rather than reaction.

Another critical aspect of future-proofing loyalty is the integration of digital and physical experiences. As e-commerce continues to dominate, customers still crave human connection, sensory engagement, and in-person interactions with brands. Businesses that successfully blend digital convenience with tangible experiences will cultivate deeper loyalty. Retailers that incorporate AR (augmented reality) and VR (virtual reality) to enhance the online shopping experience, restaurants that use digital loyalty programs to reward in-store visits, and brands that create hybrid events that merge online, and offline engagement will stand out in an increasingly digital world. Future loyalty programs will need to adapt to omnichannel lifestyles, ensuring that customers feel recognized and rewarded no matter where or how they interact with a brand.

Sustainability, ethics, and social responsibility will play an even greater role in customer loyalty moving forward. Consumers today, especially the younger generations, are making purchasing decisions based on a brand's environmental impact, labor practices, and corporate values. Businesses that fail to align with these concerns risk alienating a growing segment of conscious consumers who prioritize ethical spending. Brands that integrate sustainability into their loyalty programs such as offering incentives for eco-friendly purchases, implementing donation-based rewards, or supporting social causes through customer engagement will create value-driven loyalty that goes beyond transactions. Customers want to feel that their loyalty contributes to something meaningful, and brands that can authentically demonstrate their commitment to positive change will earn deeper emotional investment from their audience.

Another key trend shaping the future of loyalty is the rise of membership-based models. Subscription-based businesses have demonstrated the power of recurring engagement, but membership-driven loyalty goes beyond just automatic payments. Companies that create exclusive, experience-driven memberships that offer continuous value, personalization, and community-building will develop stronger, more enduring customer relationships. Brands like Amazon Prime, Netflix, and luxury concierge services have set the standard for this, but the model can be applied across industries. A beauty brand, for instance, could offer a members-only skincare consultation program, providing personalized recommendations, early product access, and VIP treatment. A travel company could introduce a global explorer membership, offering curated travel experiences, hidden destination guides, and special discounts for loyal customers. Membership-based loyalty will be about creating unique, lifestyle-driven value that makes customers feel part of something bigger than just a rewards program.

Customer advocacy will also play a central role in loyalty strategies for the future. Word-of-mouth marketing has always been powerful, but in the digital age, customers now have platforms to amplify their experiences to larger audiences. Businesses that encourage user-generated content, social proof, and community-driven brand advocacy will cultivate stronger relationships. The future of loyalty will be built on authentic brand storytelling, where customers themselves become the ambassadors, influencers, and narrators of a brand's success. Instead of relying on paid promotions, companies will empower their most passionate customers to share their experiences, reviews, and testimonials in ways that feel natural and unforced. This organic advocacy will be more persuasive and enduring than any marketing campaign.

Trust will remain the foundation of long-term loyalty, but maintaining trust in the future will require radical transparency. Customers are growing more skeptical of brands that make vague promises or engage in deceptive marketing practices. Companies that offer clear, honest communication about their products, services, pricing, and policies will build trust-based loyalty that withstands market fluctuations. Brands that provide customer-first policies, fair pricing models, and open conversations about company practices will earn long-term confidence from their audience. Future loyalty strategies will not just be about offering benefits, they will be about earning and maintaining customer respect.

As technology advances, businesses must also ensure that data privacy remains a priority in their loyalty efforts. Customers are willing to share personal information when they see tangible benefits, but they also expect control, security, and ethical usage of their data. Brands that offer privacy-first loyalty experiences, giving customers the option to manage their data, opt out of tracking, and customize their privacy settings, will stand out. Future loyalty programs will need to be transparent about data collection and usage, ensuring that customers feel empowered rather than exploited.

Ultimately, the brands that future-proof customer loyalty will be those that continuously innovate, listen to their customers, and adapt with agility. They will recognize that loyalty is not a static achievement but an evolving relationship that must be nurtured with relevance, authenticity, and value-driven engagement. Businesses that succeed will be the ones that remain customer-obsessed, anticipate change before it happens, and create experiences that make customers feel valued beyond transactions. The future of loyalty belongs to those who embrace the changing world while staying true to the fundamental human desire for connection, trust, and belonging.

The future of customer loyalty is not about maintaining the status quo but about continuous adaptation. The businesses that will thrive are those that understand that loyalty is not a given, it must be earned and re-earned in an ever-changing world. With advancements in technology, shifting consumer expectations, and growing competition, businesses must remain agile, forward-thinking, and customer-obsessed to secure long-term loyalty. Future-proofing customer loyalty requires a mindset that embraces constant evolution, deep emotional connection, and an unwavering commitment to value creation.

One of the biggest challenges in sustaining customer loyalty is consumer empowerment. Customers today are more informed, connected, and vocal than ever before. They can research alternatives, compare prices, and access peer reviews in seconds. This means that businesses can no longer rely on traditional brand loyalty; instead, they must actively engage, delight, and prove their worth to customers consistently. Brands that assume customers will remain loyal simply because of past satisfaction risk losing them to competitors who offer better experiences, more transparency, or deeper emotional connections.

For businesses to remain relevant in the future, they must shift from a transactional approach to loyalty to an experiential one. Loyalty will no longer be measured by the number of purchases a customer makes but by the depth of engagement, the frequency of meaningful interactions, and the emotional connection customers feel with a brand. The brands that foster genuine relationships will have a significant competitive advantage because emotional loyalty is harder to break than habit-based or incentive-driven loyalty.

One of the ways businesses can strengthen emotional loyalty is by aligning with customer values. Consumers today, especially younger generations, are increasingly making purchasing decisions based on ethics, sustainability, and corporate responsibility. A brand's stance on social issues, environmental impact, and ethical business practices can significantly influence customer perception and long-term loyalty. Companies that fail to align with their customers' values risk alienating them, while brands that take a stand and operate transparently build trust-based loyalty that goes beyond price and convenience.

The rise of community-driven loyalty is another critical factor shaping the future. Customers no longer just want to buy from brands; they want to be part of something bigger. Businesses that foster customer communities, peer interactions, and shared experiences create stronger bonds than those that rely solely on rewards programs. Successful brands will move away from the old model of one-way communication and instead embrace two-way dialogue, co-creation, and community engagement. This means actively listening to customers, involving them in brand decisions, and creating spaces where they can connect with like-minded individuals who share their interests, passions, or lifestyle preferences.

Technology will continue to play a transformative role in customer loyalty, but businesses must use it to enhance—not replace—human connection. While automation, AI, and machine learning enable brands to scale personalization, they must be careful not to lose the emotional depth of human interactions. Customers still value authenticity, and brands that overly rely on AI-generated engagement without a genuine human touch may find their relationships feeling hollow and impersonal. The most successful businesses will find a balance between automation and personalized human interactions, ensuring that technology enhances the customer experience rather than diminishing it.

Another critical aspect of future-proofing loyalty is seamless omnichannel integration. Customers today expect a unified, consistent experience across all touchpoints—whether they are shopping in-store, engaging via mobile apps, browsing on a website, or interacting on social media. A customer should be able to start a conversation with a brand on one platform and continue it on another without friction. Businesses that create fluid, connected experiences that transition effortlessly between digital and physical interactions will maintain stronger customer relationships. Brands that fail to integrate their channels risk frustrating customers and pushing them toward competitors who offer smoother, more convenient experiences.

One of the most significant disruptors of customer loyalty in the future will be blockchain technology and decentralized loyalty programs. Traditional loyalty programs often suffer from complexity, lack of transparency, and limited transferability, which frustrates customers. Blockchain has the potential to revolutionize loyalty systems by making rewards programs more flexible, transparent, and interoperable across multiple brands. Instead of customers being locked into a single brand's program, they could earn and redeem points across different businesses within an ecosystem. This decentralized approach would increase the perceived value of loyalty programs, making them more attractive and effective in retaining customers.

Personalization will continue to be a dominant force in loyalty strategies, but the future of personalization will be driven by deep, contextual understanding rather than surface-level customization. Businesses will need to move beyond simple name-based personalization and focus on delivering value at precisely the right moment. AI-driven insights will allow brands to anticipate when a customer is most receptive to engagement, what kind of messaging resonates best, and which experiences create the highest emotional impact. Personalization will not just be about suggesting products but about understanding customer intent, preferences, and life stages in a way that feels natural and intuitive.

Trust will remain the most important currency of loyalty. Customers will continue to favor brands that prioritize data security, ethical marketing practices, and genuine transparency. With increasing concerns about privacy, surveillance, and data misuse, businesses must go beyond just compliance with regulations; they must actively demonstrate a commitment to protecting customer information. Brands that offer customers more control over their data explain how it is being used and allow them to opt into personalized experiences rather than forcing them into data tracking systems will earn long-term credibility and trust.

Future-proofing customer loyalty requires businesses to move beyond traditional engagement strategies and embrace new paradigms of relationship-building. With rapid advancements in technology and shifting consumer behaviors, companies that remain static will inevitably lose ground to those that continuously innovate and adapt. The future belongs to brands that view customer loyalty not as a one-time achievement but as a dynamic, evolving relationship that must be nurtured consistently.

10.1 The Emotional Economy: Building Lasting Bonds Beyond Transactions

One of the most critical shifts in customer loyalty is the transition from transactional loyalty to emotional loyalty. Consumers today are driven by more than just discounts, reward points, or convenience. They seek brands that align with their personal values, evoke strong emotions, and create experiences that feel meaningful. Businesses that focus solely on providing financial incentives risk becoming interchangeable, as competitors can always offer better deals. However, brands that build emotional connections create loyalty that is far stronger than any promotion or discount could achieve.

Emotional loyalty is rooted in trust, authenticity, and personal connection. Customers remain loyal to brands that make them feel valued, respected, and understood. Companies that master the art of storytelling, humanized brand communication, and genuine customer appreciation will cultivate deep-seated emotional loyalty that withstands market fluctuations and competitive pressures. Businesses must go beyond merely selling products and instead focus on creating narratives that customers want to be a part of. A skincare brand, for example, that shares customer transformation stories and engages users in self-care education will develop a community-driven emotional bond rather than a transactional relationship.

Another crucial aspect of emotional loyalty is brand purpose and ethical alignment. Customers today, particularly the younger generations, are increasingly making purchasing decisions based on a brand's stance on social issues, sustainability, and ethical responsibility.

A company that actively champions causes that matter to its customers will build loyalty through shared values rather than just product offerings. The key is authenticity—customers can quickly detect performative activism or marketing-driven social responsibility. Businesses that integrate genuine, long-term commitments to social impact into their brand identity will attract and retain customers who align with their mission.

The emotional economy also requires brands to humanize customer interactions. With automation and AI becoming more prevalent, it is easy for customer interactions to feel robotic and impersonal. While technology enhances efficiency, it should never replace the warmth of human connection. Businesses that incorporate real, empathetic human interactions into their customer engagement strategy, whether through live support, personalized follow-ups, or community-driven conversations will create lasting impressions that reinforce loyalty.

10.2 The Role of Gamification and Habit-Forming Engagement in Loyalty

One of the most effective yet underutilized strategies for future-proofing customer loyalty is gamification and habit-forming engagement. Human psychology is wired for reward systems, milestones, and incremental progress, making gamification an incredibly powerful tool for long-term retention. Brands that incorporate interactive, achievement-based engagement models will cultivate deeper loyalty by turning brand interaction into a habitual experience rather than a one-time purchase decision.

Gamification involves integrating game-like elements—such as challenges, points, progress tracking, badges, leaderboards, and milestone rewards—into a customer's journey. This technique is particularly effective in industries where engagement is key to customer retention, such as fitness, education, finance, and entertainment. A fitness brand that tracks progress, rewards users for hitting workout milestones, and creates competitive community challenges will see higher engagement and long-term stickiness. A personal finance app that rewards users with consistent savings habits or smart spending choices will foster habitual brand reliance.

Habit formation is one of the most powerful drivers of customer retention. Brands that integrate themselves into daily routines eliminate the need for customers to consciously choose them each time, they simply become part of their lifestyle. This principle is why streaming platforms like Netflix and Spotify thrive; they are deeply embedded in daily entertainment habits. Similarly, businesses that can ingrain themselves into their customers' habits, whether through daily app usage, recurring purchases, or automated engagement loops—will create loyalty that is subconscious and enduring.

Subscription-based businesses have leveraged the habit of psychology to create continuous engagement. The key to sustaining subscription-based loyalty is to constantly provide new value that reinforces the habit of staying subscribed. Companies like Amazon Prime, which continually add benefits such as streaming, faster shipping, and exclusive deals, ensure that customers feel a growing return on investment, making cancellation less likely. The most successful businesses will continue rethinking how they can create habit loops within their engagement models, ensuring that customers do not just purchase but continue interacting with the brand on a recurring basis.

REVIEWS

"Creating Value: Winning Customer Loyalty and Trust" is not just a book; it is a masterclass on what truly drives business success in today's competitive world. As an entrepreneur who has built multiple businesses from the ground up, I can confidently say that customer trust and loyalty are the two most valuable assets any business can have. Nurudeen Adeola Akande does an exceptional job of breaking down the principles of value creation in a way that is both insightful and actionable. This book is a must-read for every business owner who wants to build a brand that stands the test of time.

Chinedu Okafor – Entrepreneur & Business Consultant

In an era where consumers are bombarded with endless choices, only brands that create real value can earn lasting customer loyalty. Nurudeen Adeola Akande captures this truth brilliantly in *Creating Value: Winning Customer Loyalty and Trust*. As someone who has worked in marketing for over a decade, I found the book incredibly relevant, especially in its discussion on emotional connections, authenticity, and trust-building. The real-world examples and strategies provided in this book make it an invaluable resource for professionals across different industries.

Aisha Bello – Marketing Director, Leading FMCG Brand

In the fast-paced world of tech startups, where growth is often prioritized over customer relationships, this book serves as a much-needed reminder that sustainable success is built on trust. *Creating Value* changed the way I approach customer engagement in my company. The book is full of practical, non-nonsense strategies that any entrepreneur or business leader can implement immediately. Nurudeen Adeola Akande has written a book that is not just relevant today but will remain timeless in its principles.

Tolu Adeniran – Tech Startup Founder

Trust is the foundation of every successful business, especially in industries like banking and finance, where customers are incredibly cautious about where they put their money. This book does an outstanding job of explaining how businesses can consistently exceed customer expectations and create an environment of transparency, reliability, and trust. What I love most is how it goes beyond theory—every chapter provides actionable strategies that can be applied in real-life scenarios. If you work in customer service, this book is a goldmine.

Fatima Yusuf – Customer Experience Manager, Financial Sector

Running a retail business in Nigeria is not easy, especially with customers constantly looking for better deals elsewhere. But after reading *Creating Value: Winning Customer Loyalty and Trust*, I realized that price wars are not the answer—creating unforgettable experiences is. This book has completely changed how I interact with my customers. The insights into exceeding expectations, building relationships, and fostering loyalty are some of the bests I've ever come across. Nurudeen

Adeola Akande has written a game-changing book, and I highly recommend it to anyone serious about business success.

Adewale Johnson – Retail Business Owner